TESTIMONIALS FOR RECOVERING YOUR PURPOSE IN A CONFUSED WORLD

I want to thank the Lord for this book. I know that it will be a true blessing for this generation. They need to have the identity and purpose given to us from eternity revealed to them. I believe that this book did not come into your hands by coincidence, but because the purpose of God is about to be revealed in your life.

I bless the life of Prophetess and Pastor Zuleyka Salazar for being a bridge of salvation to this humanity through obedience, by expressing through this book her powerful experience with the Holy Spirit, leading us clearly to the existence and the power of God.

I believe this book will be an activation for your life, since each page will make sense of your existence, due to the words that have undoubtedly come from the heart of God.

I have had the pleasure of meeting Zuleyka at a key moment in her life. It has been a life fulfilling privilege to be a prophetic mentor and I am fully convinced that this book will heal, restore, liberate, and resurrect his chosen ones.

Pastor and Prophetess Sabrina Malvina
RDG Ministerio Profetico-Argentina

I have seen how Prophetess Zuleyka Salazar has encouraged and helped many women. I have seen the process she has gone through and the transformation she has had through the power of God.

Apostol Johana Ramos

Eternal Life Embassy

Lorton, VA

A year and a half ago I met my sister and friend Prophet Zuleyka Salazar and it has been a great blessing every time she has been with our church and women's ministry. She has contributed words of comfort, wisdom, and prophecy!!! Thank you for letting yourself be used as a vessel to bless many!!! She has always given a word of empowerment to our church and prophetic revelation!!! Go ahead, there is still a lot to do. We love you. And this book is the first of many.

Pastora Carmen Diaz

Iglesia Milagros de Jesucristo

Oxon Hill, MD

I have the utmost honor to witness the prophetic unction, the spiritual gifts, and most importantly, the fruits of the Holy Spirit that testify of Zuleyka Salazar's character, which in turn has made a difference in my life and the life of many. Before Christ came into my life, I made poor decisions that had a detrimental impact on my family. I struggled with guilt, shame, anger, and regret because of that. God has used Prophetess Zuleyka Salazar to remove the anger that plagued me and imparted into me God's peace and a clarity that absolved me from the guilt, shame, and regret. God used her testimony to build my faith and have a change of perspective. Where I use to see a situation through the eyes of despair, I now see it with hope. The same way God has used her to bring freedom and peace to my mind is the same way I believe that this book that she birthed will bring to you.

Prophetess Zuleyka Salazar has been a role model in my life ever since I met her. Through her, I have learned boldness and resiliency. She is truly a blessing and someone I admire greatly.

If you are reading this literary work I guarantee you that the anointing and the weight of glory that Pastor and Prophet Zuleyka Salazar carries will be transferred to your life and your family. Because she has embodied in each chapter and each paragraph of this book a part of her life experience, that will empower many people to be raised from that place where they could not get up from for years.

Pastor and Prophet Zuleyka have been a great blessing to our people, both our Spanish-speaking and English-speaking community. Her willingness to obey the call of God has not gone unrewarded, and for that reason we see how God can use anyone without limits only if they are deposited in his hands.

Let's enjoy every expression of this book and let the Holy Spirit minister to every area of our life.

Pastor Kibsaim Jimenez, Iglesia Tabernaculo de Adoracion

ZULEYKA SALAZAR

RECOVERING YOUR *Purpose*

IN A CONFUSED WORLD

DEDICATION

To the Absolute owner of my life, my King, Lord and Savior Jesus Christ. He chose me according to his will and for the fulfillment of his purpose on Earth. Thank you, Lord, for giving me the highest honor by allowing me to serve you with my life. I love you, Jesus.

To my husband, Adinsson J. Salazar, for believing in me and giving me his continuous support, and for serving as a source of motivation and support in every aspect of my life.

To my children, my treasures, Stephanie Marie Salazar, Yamilet Angelie Salazar, Adinsson Jhayr Salazar Jr., and Valeria Elianie Salazar, for their unconditional love, understanding and for being part of the ministry that God has entrusted to us.

ACKNOWLEDGEMENTS

Once upon a time in my early Christian walk, I questioned, "Is this all the kingdom of God is about?" I felt stuck until one day, I encountered a great woman of God who removed the veil of religion I had on. She is Dr. Cindy Trimm. I attended her Kingdom School of Ministry, and she taught about the kingdom of God, and I said WOW! I knew there was more! I was excited to know that our God is great and that he has great plans for those who trust and believe in him. Attending this school helped me understand that there is more. I felt like I was set free. I walked out of the cave of darkness and slavery, and was removed from prison. I found purpose, and what I am sharing with you are some tools that God gifted me to support others who cannot find their purpose and who are stuck in their own caves.

I also want to give special thanks to Margarita Cruz Velez, the woman that God used as a channel to bring me into the world. She is not only an excellent mother, but also a great friend. Thank you, Mom, for your wise advice, unconditional support, and always covering us with your prayers.

I want to share my sincere gratitude to the many men and women of God who have inspired us; to my mentors, friends, fellow ministers, and all those who have contributed in some way so that God's dream may flourish in our lives.

I want to thank the family of Eternal Life Embassy for believing in the ministry God has given us by grace. You are all very special, and I pray that God continues leading us to the fulfillment of our purpose as a church family. We are overcomers!

FOREWORD

Life has not been a crystal staircase; I still remember the day my wife and I met at Wakefield High School. She was 17 when we had our first daughter. She pushed through high school with her big belly and received multiple scholarships, but knew that I wanted to go to school, so she took a step back for me to pursue my career. The woman I am speaking about has stuck with me through bankruptcy, going from our own townhouse to living in her aunt's apartment, sleeping on two sofas, having a closet filled with our belongings in black trash bags, and my chest being our daughter's crib. Sadness, poverty, stress, and depression had wrapped us up in such a way that we could see no way out of this depreciating cave of sorrow.

Living in a place that is too dark to see clearly is the same as being in a place that is too dark to live. *Recovering Your Purpose in a Confused World* is a book that will give you a plan for a 180-degree change in your life. It is not based on a fairy tale; it is a living testimony of what God can do when you yield to him, especially when no one else can help you.

I can attest to the miraculous change in the life of my wife, as her closest witness. I first-hand observed God molding my wife into the woman of God that she is today. This book embodies the very essence of the Holy Spirit, who has been key in the transformation of my wife's life, and will guide you in overcoming the assassins of your purpose. In this book, my wife will take you through a journey that will give you initiative, faith, and the will to win in life. You will end up experiencing a metamorphic change to get the results God has planned for you.

Pastor Adinsson J. Salazar

Vice President at E.L.E Ministries

FOREWORD

The late Dr. Myles Munroe once said, *"The graveyard is the richest place on the surface of the earth because there you will see the books that were not published, ideas that were not harnessed, songs that were not sung, and drama pieces that were never acted."* What a powerful statement! How many times have we got stuck in a place where we imagined our way out of our God's best purpose for our lives? How many times have we thought about what it would be like if things were just different? Are we going to seed the graveyard with our purpose, or are we going to let the world enjoy who God called us to be?

In my xperience, I've encountered so many talented individuals that were not living up to their full potential. These individuals *seemed to be alive, but not living.* They reached a certain level of comfort where their circumstances limited their joy and prohibited them from achieving their dreams. I have seen many great men and women settle for less than what they were designed to be. What's unsettling about this is that they knew it. They knew that God had called them for much more, but something was holding them back. Something fed into their fears. There was something disastrous hidden in their subconscious, and some of them could not even pinpoint the issue.

I believe that Zuleyka Salazar, through divine revelation, goes into the deepest part of our soul to help us identify the issue, heal, and uproot it. Zuleyka, through her own life experiences and practical teachings, takes us on a journey of recovery. It's not the easiest journey to travel, but it's extremely necessary to live a life of purpose. *Recovering Your Purpose in a Confused World* is the mirror that we need to get us on the pathway to a breakthrough.

I have personally seen Zuleyka's journey from childhood to the woman of God she has become. What a transformation! What you will read in these pages is not just a theory, but the truth that set her free and gave her the power to write about it. Now it is your turn.

The days of walking around wondering why you are in this world are over! Hallelujah!

Apostle Henry Ramos

Apostle at Eternal Life Embassy

President of E.L.E. Ministries

TABLE OF CONTENTS

INTRODUCTION

During the process of writing my book, I reflected on my life and was astonished by the incredible power of God that transformed me. I was amazed by what God accomplished with me, a person who simply placed trust in him and believed in his words for my life. Furthermore, it was even more significant to comprehend that God knew me even before my physical existence. Initially, I struggled to accept that I was valued by God due to my past experiences.

Adversely, there is someone influencing the decisions we make, and he wants the destruction of all mankind. He is Satan, and his priority is to corrupt God's original design for our lives. His assignment is to break up relationships and wreak havoc between families, communities, industries, educational systems, and people all over the world. The enemy wants to confuse and destroy the purpose God has placed in you. This book illustrates how light can overcome the darkness. You do not need to live a life of resentment, regret, or sadness. In John 8:12, Jesus states, *"I am the light of the world. Whoever follows me will never walk in darkness, but will have the light of life."* Beloved, if you follow Jesus, darkness has no control over your life!

I believe you will be invigorated, renewed, and strengthened by every chapter of this book! I have been able to translate and summarize the critical, transformative life that Christ has enabled me to live because of following him. Understand that rejection, pain, sadness, loneliness, betrayal, self-hatred, and failure are not the end of your story. God will restore your identity and he will lead you back to your purpose. This book will remind you that you are born to experience the magnificent power of God, and go from glory to glory as you pursue all that he has for you in the light of his love!

CHAPTER 1

CAVE OF THE MIND

The question arises whether there exists a broader perspective of life than what has been encountered till now. At the time of our conception, we were influenced by our genetic makeup, based on our parents' DNA. Subsequently, we were brought up according to certain beliefs and values, which have contributed to shaping our current outlook. While some individuals have overcome life's adversities and become stronger, others have been weakened by them.

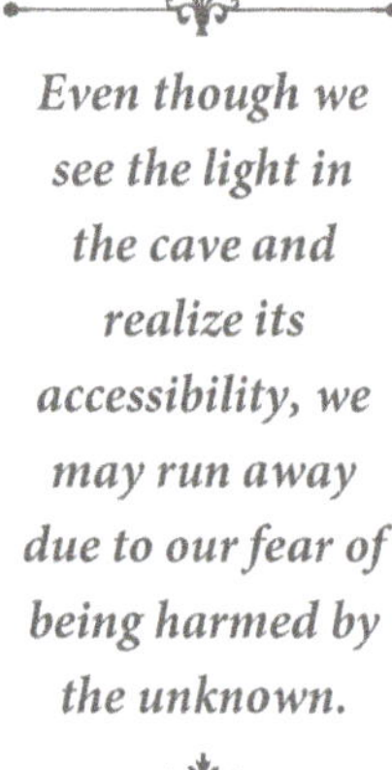

Even though we see the light in the cave and realize its accessibility, we may run away due to our fear of being harmed by the unknown.

At this moment, some of us may be experiencing a "cave" existence. A cave is a natural void in the ground, specifically a space large enough for a human. It feels dark, cold, stuffy, and humid with little or no oxygen. For some, it is a safe place where no one can be hurt. A place where no one is invited, and many have been scared away. This cave mentality has become a haven for many. A home away from home. This pseudo home has become a place of refuge where you are the only one welcomed. As desirable as that may sound, it can become a place of destruction, loss, and catastrophe. Even though the cave feels safe, it is not safe. That cave is the same place where the sudden appearance of an unknown light may bring an uneasy feeling, a threat. Even though we see the light in the cave and realize its accessibility, we may run away due to our fear of being harmed by the unknown.

Our life experiences and circumstances placed us into the cave. Darkness was our norm until a spark of light revealed that there was much more to life. We were spiritually designed to operate from above the cave, not inside the cave! Jesus had this to say about dwelling on a rock:

And Jesus answered him, "Blessed are you, Simon Bar-Jonah! For flesh and blood has not revealed this to you, but my Father who is in heaven. And I tell you, you are Peter, and on this rock[a] I will build my church, and the gates of hell[b] shall not prevail against it. I will give you the keys of the kingdom of heaven, and whatever you bind on earth shall be bound in heaven, and whatever you loose on earth shall be loosed in heaven."

MATTHEW 16:17-19 (ESV)

This verse tells us that Jesus is the rock. He is building the church on top of it so the gates of Hell will not prevail. Being on top of the rock means that you will enjoy everything the Lord has prepared for you. When you are in the cave, you may unknowingly submit yourself to experiencing a life of bondage and darkness. That was not God's intent for your life!

The darkness that surrounds us can often be traced back to the environment created by our ancestors, which we have inherited. This cultural inheritance may be invisible to us and accepted as normal, but it is merely a facade that keeps us from the truth. God's original plan for our lives does not include this "normal" state. The truth can be found in the Holy Bible, which is the Word of our Creator. However, the darkness that envelops us is like being in a cave that prevents us from discovering the truth.

Upon exiting the cave, you will recognize the significance of abiding on the rock, which represents Jesus Christ. Being atop the rock allows you to envision and achieve feats that may seem impossible, with the help of Christ. Your thoughts and capabilities expand, and you become victorious beyond measure. By establishing Jesus as the cornerstone of your life, you come to understand that there is more to life than what you have experienced in the past or present. You acknowledge that good prevails over evil by recognizing the supremacy of God's goodness over all else.

A common issue is that many people choose to remain in their own personal cave. They might think that it is more comfortable and secure to hide away rather than expose themselves to the outside world. Often, individuals do not want to reveal their inner state. They may believe that the cave is the best place to avoid being hurt by others or anything else, but they fail to realize the potential danger it poses. Your biggest adversary is yourself because you have full access to all aspects of your life. It is crucial to be rescued by accepting the gift of salvation offered by Jesus Christ as soon as possible. Without help, your life could turn into a catastrophic event. You must focus on your inner self and have faith in the person of Jesus Christ to bask in the light of his love and surrender to its safety.

It has been my observation that some people have faith in others, but do not have enough faith in themselves. You must prioritize the journey of self-recovery in order to be authentically available for the greater work that God has called you to. The prophet Elijah had enough faith to do the work of God, but lacked faith when it came to himself.

> *There he came to a cave and lodged in it. And behold, the word of the Lord came to him, and he said to him, "What are you doing here, Elijah?" He said, "I have been very jealous for the Lord, the God of hosts. For the people of Israel have forsaken your covenant, thrown down your altars, and killed your prophets with the sword, and I, even I only, am left, and they seek my life, to take it away."*
>
> **1 KINGS 19:9-10 (ESV)**

Elijah, a man who was threatened by Queen Jezebel's intentions of killing him, sought refuge in a cave due to his fear of her ability to follow through with her word. Despite being aware of the Lord's presence, his response was to hide away in a place of safety. This is an example of how the words and actions of others can create a sense of fear and uncertainty, causing one to retreat from unfamiliar or potentially dangerous situations.

Prophet Elijah did not have enough faith to believe that God would protect him, so he hid from life in a cave of depression. He was intimidated by the idea of being the only prophet alive, not knowing more prophets existed. 7,000 other prophets had not bowed their knees to Baal. The idea of going through life alone creates a victim mindset, killing dreams and all other possibilities. A person with a victim mentality who has suffered through trauma

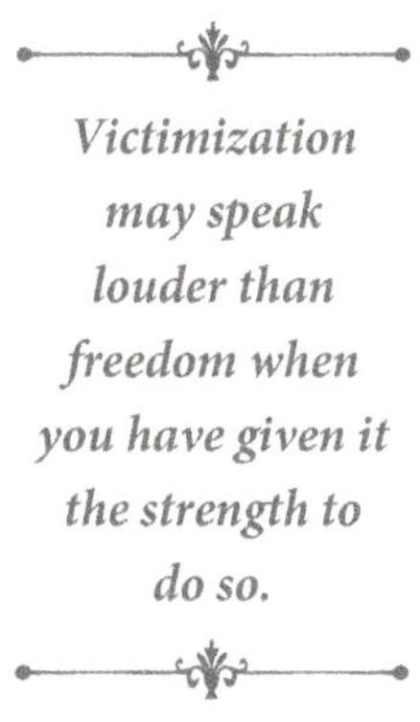

Victimization may speak louder than freedom when you have given it the strength to do so.

or tribulations may not have developed a healthier way to cope. This mentality promotes feelings of negativity, no matter the situation. These individuals continuously operate under the assumption that everyone is after them. In other words, someone with this mindset constantly feels that they are the target; they expect to be offended. It is difficult to see the light of joy, hope, and love come into your life if you think this way. Victimization may speak louder than freedom when you have given it the strength to do so. But God…their saving grace comes from a higher place. Battles are fought in the heavenly places so that the victory can be experienced here on earth. The question is, do you believe? Or are you like the Prophet Elijah caught up in your circumstances?

²¹ So He asked his father, "How long has this been happening to him?" And he said, "From childhood. ²² And often he has thrown him both into the fire and into the water to destroy him. But if You can do anything, have compassion on us and help us."

²³ Jesus said to him, "If[d] you can believe, all things are possible to him who believes."

²⁴ Immediately the father of the child cried out and said with tears, "Lord, I believe; help my unbelief!"

MARK 9:21-24 (NKJV)

My cave experience began in my childhood.

Throughout my childhood, I faced a multitude of difficulties with my father, which resulted in feelings of self-rejection, dishonesty, a lack of self-identity, and a sense of being lost. Even before I was born, my father rejected me due to my gender, as he believed only men could produce male offspring. This belief, which was reinforced by my grandfather, caused my father to distance himself from me. When I was born, my father abandoned my mother at the hospital and showed no remorse for his actions. Despite having a son prior to my birth, my father's happiness was short-lived, as he continued to physically and mentally abuse my mother. Her courage to leave him ultimately led to her departure with three children, with me being the middle child and only daughter.

At the age of six, my mother made the decision to relocate our family to the United States with the belief that it would provide opportunities for us to become successful world leaders. She had a selfless desire to serve others and contribute to the country she had grown fond of. However, upon arrival, my mother remarried a man from a different cultural background who had a mindset that clashed with our own cultural beliefs. He was financially stingy and physically and mentally abusive towards me and my older brother. He would frequently insult me by calling me "stupid" and once even caused me to be unable to walk due to the severity of the beating he inflicted upon me. It was a shocking realization that we were once again in an abusive environment, similar to the one we had left behind in Puerto Rico. Despite the abuse not being directed towards her, my mother immediately left him upon discovering the ongoing mistreatment towards myself and my brother.

She became a single mother of three and gave us the best life she could ever offer us, which I'm highly grateful for. Meanwhile, my father would call us from Puerto Rico every now and then, but our relationship was never a loving one. Even though our mother did everything she could to make things right, it was too late for me. During my teen years, I decided to enter a dark mental cave to escape the impact of the trauma I experienced from the abuse. The darkness of the cave became my comfort zone; it became a place of rest where my truth was my truth, and no one could say otherwise. If anyone tried to challenge my truths and tried to remove me from my comfort zone, I would protect myself by verbally and physically abusing others and bullying them.

God has an answer for our cave experience!

Even though my cave was a place of comfort for me, it limited my eyesight by blurring my vision, affecting my education and mobilization. I knew there was more for me, but anger, rage, deception, and bitterness kept me inside the cave, my comfort zone. My protective instincts left me with limited happiness and little satisfaction. One day when I was in my cave, a dark shadow appeared. It reflected the darkness of my soul. It became everything that I was missing: my father, my best friend, my adviser, and my brothers. The shadow eventually got so big that it engulfed me and brought me a false assurance. I became comfortable in this place until the responsibility for another human life moved me take a closer look at where I was.

When I became a young mother I began to search for answers outside of my cave experience. One day I was invited to go to church by my mother. I reluctantly accepted the invitation. During the service, I heard a worship song that literally changed my life. The words of the song said, *"Separated from You, I am nothing, away from You I die. If You are not in me, I despair. I lose hope, and I lose my desire for life."* Those very words penetrated the darkness of my cave like resistance and a flicker of light brightened the inside of the cave. The veil of my iniquity was lifted, my truth was exposed for the lie it was and I noticed that I was all alone in chains. I realized my cave of false security and comfort was hiding my God ordained destiny. I was unaware that I was gambling with my destiny by seeking a false sense of security for my life's emotional and psychological traumas.

Here's a more formal definition for what I was experiencing:

<u>Emotional trauma</u> is the end result of events or experiences that leave us feeling deeply unsafe and often helpless. It is the result of extraordinarily stressful events that shatter your sense of security, making you feel helpless in a dangerous world.

<u>Psychological trauma</u> can leave you struggling with upsetting emotions, memories, and anxiety that won't go away. It can also leave you feeling numb, disconnected, and unable to trust other people.

Now, childhood trauma can result from anything that disrupts a child's sense of safety, including:

- ➢ An unstable or unsafe environment
- ➢ Separation from a parent
- ➢ Serious illness
- ➢ Intrusive medical procedures
- ➢ <u>Sexual, physical, or verbal abuse</u>
- ➢ Domestic violence
- ➢ Neglect

During the first trimester of my mother's pregnancy when the doctor told my mother I was a girl, my father became increasingly verbally abusive towards her. The security of my mother's womb (a dark place like a cave) was threatened by his aggressive disapproval of my gender. This initially planted the seeds for my emotional demise in my heart of hearts. It has been scientifically proven that an embryo is sensitive to its outer surroundings. In her article, *Babies Learn to Recognize Words in the Womb*, Beth Skwarecki states, "It may seem implausible that fetuses can listen to speech within the womb, but the sound-processing parts of their brain become active in the last trimester of pregnancy, and sound carries fairly well through the mother's abdomen.[1]

---

[1] Skwareck, B. (2013, August 26). *Babies learn to recognize words in the womb.* Science. Retrieved 2023, American Association for the Advancement of Science, from
https://www.science.org/content/article/babies-learn-recognize-words-womb. Doi: 10.1126/article.24273

'If you put your hand over your mouth and speak, that's very similar to the situation the fetus is in,' says cognitive neuroscientist Eino Partanen of the University of Helsinki. 'You can hear the rhythm of speech, rhythm of music, and so on.'"[2]

In my additional research I found the following proof that the negative words of my father influenced my destiny. *When Can My Unborn Baby Hear Me?*, written by Jennifer Shy, pediatrician at Children's Medical group in Atlanta, Georgia says, "At around 18 weeks of pregnancy, your unborn baby will start being able to hear sounds in your body like your heartbeat. At 27 to 29 weeks (6 to 7 months), they can hear some sounds outside your body too, like your voice. By the time they are full term, they will be able to hear at about the same level as an adult."[3]

Even with this scientific proof, many people believe that when a baby is a fetus, they cannot be influenced by what happens outside of the womb. But God, our creator, has known us before conception. So regardless of what is spoken over us as babies in the womb, God has a good future for us. We simply have to come out of the cave of our misunderstanding to receive it. Even though my father spoke negative words over my life, that wasn't God's intent for me. When I put myself in the cave for protection, it gave God an opportunity to really show me who I was. Allow me to share something with you. Did you know when a baby is conceived that God's plan for their lives is already in motion?

---

[2] *Scientists: Brain wave patterns show unborn children recognize words in the womb.* ONEOFUS. (2017, September 28). Retrieved 2023, European Federation for Life and Human Dignity, from https://oneofus.eu/scientists-brain-wave-patterns-show-unborn-children-recognize-words-in-the-womb/#:~:text=%E2%80%9CIf%20you%20put%20your%20hand,music%2C%20and%20so%20on.%E2%80%9D

[3] (https://www.healthychildren.org/English/tips-tools/ask-the-pediatrician/Pages/I%E2%80%99m-pregnant-and-would-like-to-sing-to-my-unborn-baby.aspx#:~:text=At%20around%2018%20weeks%20of,same%20level%20as)

The bible says:

> *¹⁶ Your eyes saw my unformed body; all the days ordained for me were written in your book before one of them came to be.*
>
> **PSALM 139:16 (NIV)**

It amazes me to know that God was watching over my unformed body. He gave me form by molding me in my mother's womb. That is a powerful insight; it's encouraging to know that since the day you were conceived and given life, your Creator was present, watching you grow for 9 months, and is even now by your side. WOW! Acknowledging this truth that took place brings such indescribable joy. We must open the eyes of our understanding to see the spiritual and mental development that occurs when a child is in the mother's womb. They are actually listening to the daily interactions of their mother. Have you seen pregnant women speak to their bellies, and the baby responds back with physical movements? When the baby is in the womb, they are very attentive to what is happening around them.

As early as conception, the enemy can use traumatic experiences such as rejection, oppression, and deceit to put you in a cave-like existence. Here are several of the emotional and psychological symptoms that one might have after experiencing trauma:

- ➢ Shock, denial, or disbelief
- ➢ Confusion, difficulty concentrating
- ➢ Anger, irritability, mood swings
- ➢ Anxiety and fear
- ➢ Guilt, shame, self-blame

- ➤ Withdrawing from others
- ➤ Feeling sad or hopeless
- ➤ Feeling disconnected or numb

Take time to examine which of these symptoms you are experiencing and identify the ones that are still threatening your emotional, physical, or spiritual well-being.

Now let's look at some physical symptoms that are connected to emotional and psychological traumas:

- ➤ Insomnia or nightmares
- ➤ Fatigue
- ➤ Being startled easily
- ➤ Difficulty concentrating
- ➤ Racing heartbeat
- ➤ Edginess and agitation
- ➤ Aches and pains
- ➤ Muscle tension

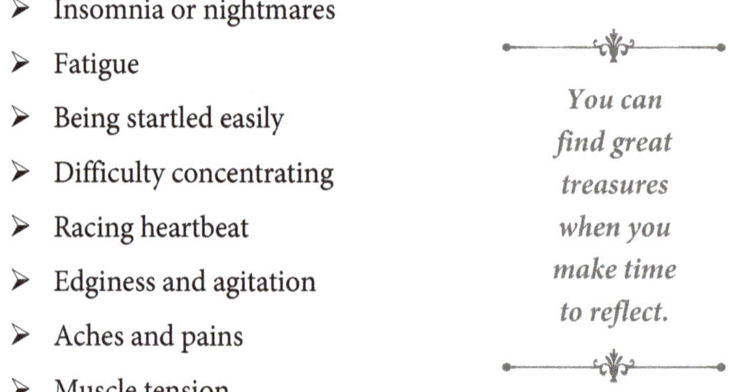

Making time for self-examination is beneficial if you are experiencing any of these symptoms and if you are serious about identifying the things that may be holding you back from the light of God's love.

You can find great treasures when you make time to reflect. Empowerment is the authority or power given to someone to do something. It can also be the process of becoming stronger and more confident, especially in controlling one's life and claiming one's rights. Acknowledging self is a kick starter to the freedom that empowers an individual. Empowerment can come in many forms: social, educational, economic, political, or psychological. When you are looking internally for treasures, you have to let go of your problems. Sometimes we spend too much time focusing on the problem and not seeking the solution. We continuously entertain ourselves with past traumas and present issues, which give us no time to encounter the treasures that our Creator has established for our freedom.

14 Guard the good deposit that was entrusted to you—guard it with the help of the Holy Spirit who lives in us.
2 TIMOTHY 1:14 (NIV)

Everything that you see and do or not see in the world has been created by someone. Henry T. Sampson created the first cell phone back in 1971. As the creator of the first cell phone, he knows how to maximize its usage. That's also true with us. Our Creator, God, has created us and He knows how to maximize the potential of every human being. He knows what we are capable of withstanding and the circumstances that we can overcome. He knows the talents, knowledge, power, and authority that he has placed in us to fulfill our purpose. Essentially, once you find out your purpose, your reason for living, you will bring hope to the world. This is why it is important to examine yourself so that you can best develop a strategy for a better life. Trust the Manufacturer and Creator of your life because He knows all the plans He has conceived for you.

For I know the plans I have for you," declares the LORD, "plans to prosper you and not to harm you, plans to give you hope and a future.
JEREMIAH 29:11 (NIV)

For the fulfillment of Jeremiah 29:11 to come to pass, you must grant Jesus access to your life through a confession of your faith in Him. By confessing that you accept him as your Lord and Savior, you have activated this scripture. The word *savior* means one that saves from danger and destruction. Another definition is someone that gives their own life for someone else's. It is important to initiate a relationship with God our Savior, to start this journey with a strong foundation. Did you notice how I use the words "grant access?" That's because He will not force anyone to do anything that violate their free will. Did you also notice that I said "initiated?" That's because it is a process, and you must be patient with God and yourself as you transform into what He purposed you to be. You will experience many different things as you make this adjustment, including a change in how you view life and self. Our Savior, Lord Jesus Christ, left his Holy Spirit to guide us on this beautiful journey. He is the light that shines into every part of our lives, equipping us with the knowledge, understanding, and wisdom to operate as a problem solver instead of being the problem. This is how we heal the land and become an asset to ourselves, families, communities, institutions, industry, the kingdom, and the world.

Life has meaning, the key is knowing who we are!

As human beings, we all have a deep desire to discover our purpose in life and to understand whether life has any meaning. This quest can be fraught with challenges and difficulties that may leave us feeling frustrated and lost. With so many complex issues facing society today, it can be even harder to establish a sense of identity that is both psychologically and socially healthy. Those who struggle with their identity may experience a range of negative symptoms, including emotional distress, strained relationships, and physical illness. Additionally, the need for external validation and approval can be a dangerous trap that ultimately leads to rejection and despair. Grammy award winning artist Lecrae puts it this way: "If you live for people's acceptance, you will die from their rejection." No matter what you do, someone will always have something negative to say. The opinion of others is like having a belly button; everyone has their own. However, the opinion of others does not overpower your own voice. Seeking people's approval is what may have gotten you into a cave full of deception and insecurities. When you seek the approval of men, you lose who you are and jeopardize your God given assignment by placing it in the wrong hands. Your journey to truth begins with self-knowledge and ends with self-mastery.

At times, people may not be aware of what they don't know. They may not have had the chance to learn how to complete a specific task or tackle a problem similar to the one they are currently facing. As a result, they may feel stuck, and those around them may not comprehend the difficulties they are experiencing in moving forward. This situation could lead to being permanently trapped in a state of ignorance. It is crucial to realize that ignorance can be a hindrance. Imagine living your entire life without ever learning, growing, or progressing. Ignorance can easily become a habit for someone. To overcome this, one must have an encounter with the Holy Spirit who can reveal one's shortcomings and bring about a shift in mindset, leading to a re-education, expansion of knowledge and understanding, and an ability to receive wisdom from God.

Let's compare two key words that are often confused in the last sentence, wisdom, and knowledge. The primary difference between the two words is that wisdom involves a healthy dose of perspective and the ability to make sound judgments about a subject, while knowledge is simply knowing. In other words, a person needs both to live a life of freedom and fruitfulness, which many desire. Knowledge is power; ignorance is weakness. Get out of ignorance and let the light guide you.

When the Holy Spirit turns on the light of God's wisdom and brings understanding our way, we must readily embrace it as the gift it is. Be careful not to misinterpret or reject the gift because it could result in being stuck in ignorance, not just for your generation, but for many generations to come.

> *My people are destroyed for lack of knowledge. Because you have rejected knowledge, I also will reject you from being priest for Me; Because you have forgotten the law of your God, I also will forget your children.*
>
> **HOSEA 4:6 (NKJV)**

Knowledge brings freedom to your children and your children's children. The more knowledge a person gains in life, the more they will prevail. Do not rationalize or justify the place you are currently in. We are constantly surrounded by deception and believe that it is truth when God has so much more wisdom available for us. Often, we rely on other things to think for us such as technology, other people, or cultural and societal norms. When we do that, we shut down the Holy Spirit and allow other influences to take control of our lives. This mindset must change in order to see the light and walk out of the cave towards our destiny.

This is the message we have heard from him and proclaim to you, that God is light, and in him is no darkness at all. If we say we have fellowship with him while we walk in darkness, we lie and do not practice the truth. But if we walk in the light, as he is in the light, we have fellowship with one another, and the blood of Jesus his Son cleanses us from all sin.

1 JOHN 1:5-7 (ESV)

Light has always been a symbol of holiness, goodness, knowledge, wisdom, grace, hope, and God's revelation. Light always involves the removal of darkness in the unfolding of biblical history and theology. By contrast, darkness has been associated with evil, sin, and despair.

The light is the Holy Spirit. When the light shines, its assignment is to bring forth everything that needs to be examined that is not contributing to you living an abundant life. It is time to allow the light to enter the cave and destroy the chains that so easily bind us to the lies of the enemy, Satan. The light has overcome darkness.

God's light that is accessible to you today, is here to reveal that you have been in the cave for far too long. It is time to come out. Every person deserves to live in freedom. Every individual deserves to be happy. The key is to understand that the light guides you outside of darkness and moves toward your purpose.

Are you ready to come out of the cave?

Can you perceive that something great is coming your way on the other side of the darkness?

¹⁹ See, I am doing a new thing! Now it springs up; do you not perceive it? I am making a way in the wilderness and streams in the wasteland.

Isaiah 43:19 (NIV)

God is ready to do something new in your life! Are you ready to walk in the light?

BRINGING IT TO THE TABLE -THE WHY?

Everything we do in life is an automatic response to a why. We might not know what the "why" is, but God knows. When I think about the word WHY, the following words come to my mind.

- ➢ What
- ➢ Has
- ➢ You

Your why is the inner cause for every outer effect. The Law of Cause-and-Effect states that good causes bring good effects, and bad causes bring bad effects. Likewise, your cause (thoughts/deeds) brings about your effect. What occupies your mind today will eventually fill your mouth, and the words you speak will eventually become a reality. James Allen, author of *As a Man Thinketh* said:

> *"The outer conditions of a person's life will always be found to be harmoniously related to his inner state...Men do not attract that which they want, but that which they are."*[4]

When you audit your thoughts, you need to keep a journal to record the thoughts that pass through your mind. You need to write down why you are having those types of thoughts to establish a thinking pattern. What seeds are attached to these thoughts that are producing either desirable or undesirable fruits? A seed is a metaphor for a thought, feeling, word, action, or anything that can reproduce itself. When you carry desirable fruits, you accelerate through doors of opportunity because everyone desires the fruits that you carry.

---

[4] https://www.goodreads.com/quotes/44457-the-outer-conditions-of-a-person-s-life-will-always-be#:~:text=%E2%80%9CThe%20outer%20conditions%20of%20a%20person%27s%20life%20will,are.%E2%80%9D%20%E2%80%95%20James%20Allen%2C%20As%20a%20Man%20Thinketh

When people go out to buy a product, they often don't buy it for what it does; they buy the *why*. Great companies don't hire skilled people and motivate them; they hire already motivated people and inspire them to learn the skill. Decisions are made based on three levels:

1. what we do
2. how we do it
3. why we do it.

It is very common for people to know what they do and how they did it, but the mystery is the *why*. To live the fullness of life, you must have all three levels. When you miss the *why*, you start losing passion for your actions. For instance, when you go to work you start losing interest, start feeling lazy, and become consistently tardy for what seemed to be your dream job. It is the same in relationships. When you initiate a relationship, your *why* seems clear, but as time passes, your *why* may start changing, and you lose your interest in your partner. When you take time to audit your *whys*, your life starts changing drastically; you start finding happiness and a passion that you had never experienced before. When you know your *why*, the filter is clear, and you have a better view of life and know when to say *no* or *yes*. You realize that your decisions have the power to bring a level of joy, patience, and wisdom to someone's life and make you a solutionist. If you don't know you're *why*, you will have a hard time figuring out someone else's *why*. Understanding someone else's *why* can help you grow in business, relationships, and many other areas of life. The key is to continually take time to self-reflect. This time will help you stay on top of your *whys* and ensure that they serve our society. Your *why* should always aim to change the world for the better.

You can do this through sharing, giving, and helping. Unfortunately, when we don't know our *why*, we end up doing the opposite.

So let's take a look at why we do what we do!

We constantly make daily decisions, but do you know why we make them? Most of the time, our decisions are made due to an internal response to an adverse circumstance which produces a negative seed. A seed is a metaphor for a thought, feeling, word, action, or anything that can reproduce itself. When a seed is planted in the soil, the seed is seeking fertilization to mature. Humans are like soil in that we are nurtured by our environments.

For example, when someone plants a seed of rejection, the seed will demand water, sun, and attention to grow, and the soil matures the seed of rejection and because its origin was bad, it will produce bad fruit.

Rebellion is often a byproduct of the bad fruit of rejection. As a pastor, I have counseled many individuals who responded with rebellion when rejected by their caregivers. You often see this especially during their teen years. This leads to self-destructive behavior that can ultimately lead to death. According to UCLA health, "Suicide is the second-leading cause of death among people age 15 to 24 in the U.S. Nearly 20% of high school students report serious thoughts of suicide and 9% have made an attempt to take their lives, according to the National Alliance on Mental Illness."[5]

Another way a seed is watered is when you compare your life with someone else's. If you grew up without a father, you may reject or desire

---

[5] https://www.uclahealth.org/news/suicide-rate-highest-among-teens-and-young-adults

someone else's father. When you watch a little child holding hands with their father, you continuously stare and contemplate, desiring to be that child and questioning why your father did not accept you. As you continue to water and give the attention the seed desires, you will start expressing anger and rage because of the rejection you are feeling. Rejection can become an infection that will blind you into believing that you will never be accepted in this world, and that can lead to serious consequences.

Examine the seeds of the heart through the light of God's love!

To live a full life of abundance and joy in all areas of our lives, we must examine the seeds that have been planted in our soil-the heart. The light of the Holy Spirit is needed to examine your soil. He can enter your heart and reveal to you the seeds that must be uprooted in order to advance in your purpose. Remember, the light is the only source that can light up places where darkness reigns.

> *23 Search me, O God, and know my heart: try me, and know my thoughts: 24 And see if there be any wicked way in me, and lead me in the way everlasting.*
>
> **PSALM 139:23-24 (KJV)**

The light will lead you to life everlasting and you will never want to go back to the cave of darkness. It is crucial that we recognize the seed, so we can become more aware of our daily decisions. When I refer to daily decisions, I'm referring to the daily habits that have taken you to the place you are now. For example, don't live a rushed life. We must learn to pause and meditate on self, which is part of self-care. How can you genuinely care for others if you don't care for yourself? The Lord left us an important commandment, and it is:

> *37 Jesus said to him, '"You shall love the LORD your God with all your heart, with all your soul, and with all your mind.' 38 This is the first and great commandment. 39 And the second is like it: ' You shall love your neighbor as yourself. '*
>
> **MATTHEW 22:37-39 (NKJV)**

This passage will help you understand the importance of self-care. It is essential to take time to get to know yourself. You must reach the level of knowing who you are in Christ and accepting it. When you dedicate time to yourself, you can truly love your neighbor and show it through acts of service. Some people do acts of service expecting something in return and believe that it is love. Love is when you decide to die to your own desires for your neighbor's benefit without expecting anything in return. When someone commits an act of kindness and the expectancy of compensation has not been expressed, this can lead to trouble due to a lack of communication. The sad part of it is that the individual who received the benefit may have no idea about this expectancy for compensation, and that's when the trouble starts. However, if this situation is approached with the God kind of love on both sides, it can be easily resolved. When you love God with all your heart, you can supernaturally love yourself and others without attributing a cost to that love.

God wants love to be our motivator for everything we do. When it comes to decision-making, the *why* (your heart motive) is important, and many of us ignore the *why*. It is important to investigate the reason you are reacting to something by checking your heart motive. Ask yourself why you are doing this, and then ask God why. Psalm 139:23 says, *Search me, God, and know my heart: test me and know my anxious thoughts.*

The Seed Motivates Your Why!

Individuals who are always in a bad mood may wonder why they can't seem to attract people to be around them. This is because their original thought or seed is negative and unappealing, like fruit that tastes bitter and unpleasant instead of sweet and delicious. The world already has enough negativity, such as anger and bitterness, but the fruits of God are different. The solution to this problem is found in the "Recovering Your Purpose in a Confused World" journey, where you will identify the negative thoughts and emotions you wish to eliminate. It is common to feel unsatisfied with oneself or one's possessions, but it is time to confront these negative feelings.

Understanding your why gives you purpose!

You may have an innate desire to accomplish many things, but because you don't know your *why*, you may feel lost. Some even lose opportunities presented to them due to fear, shame, self-condemnation, and feeling unworthy. When you know your *why*, you can override the emotional resistance that comes with it. As you examine your *whys*, you will realize that a lot of the things you do have been doing is stealing time, energy, hope, and resources from your purpose. Remember your purpose is what gives life to you. It is the reason that you exist.

When you encounter your purpose, you better understand why you exist. Our *why* is the thing we give to the world, and we must look inside ourselves to discover it. Your why is what drives you to do whatever it is that you do professionally or personally: mom, coach, teacher, police officer, etc. Knowing yourself will help you better understand your purpose and help you identify the areas that need some adjustments. For instance, the *why* is like the steering wheel on your vehicle; when steered in a certain direction the wheels of the car take you to

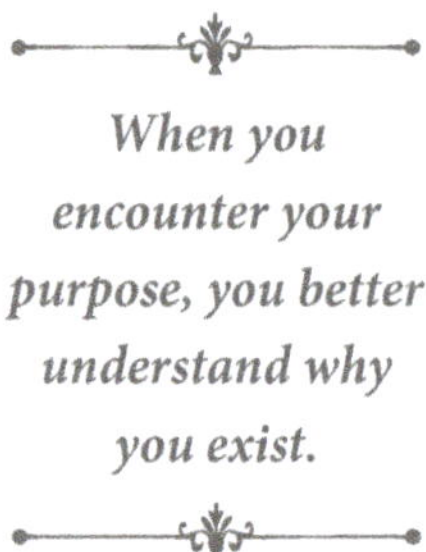

your destination. For example, whenever you are hungry, you will drive yourself to a restaurant to get something to eat. When you have bills that are due, you get a job to pay them. When you are ready to settle down and start a family, you find a wife and get married.

Your *why* is the fuel behind all the actions you take in life. It has the power to propel you to your destiny and set you free from fear and anxiety. It gives you the courage and strength to be the solution to problems. Your *why* must be in tune with the authentic you, especially when you are doing acts of service. It should never be a self-centered *why* because it limits the positive result of your actions. Your *why* drives what you do. If you are motivated for selfish gain, be it personal or for profit, it can have a negative effect on your outcome.

Seeking validation from others diminishes your why.

You are made in the image of Christ. Seeking validation from any other source diminishes your *why*. For example, in today's culture teens can get stuck in seeking approval and validation from their peers. They create a cave where the acceptance of their peers is essential to their self-image and intrinsic value. In extreme cases, this can become addictive.

There are four stages of addiction can also be applied to seeking the approval of others or being people pleasers. Here are the various stages that a teen may find themselves in as they progress in their usage.

1. *The Experimental Stage* - this is when an individual voluntarily does something, not experiencing any negative consequences, and is often accepted and encouraged because of their performance. For example: The teen may post something negative about a classmate for the first time and it gets them a lot of likes.

2. *The Occasional Usage Stage* - is when the occasional performance becomes a regular occurrence and is now part of a routine. For example: The teen may start checking their social media everyday after school before completing their homework.

3. *The High-Risk Stage* – this is when the craving for recognition and acceptance becomes unbearable, and it may drive an individual to do things they would not normally do, like sacrifice family time to be on their phones or stay shut up in their room for long periods of time.

4. *The Addiction Stage* – this is when an individual has entered into a total dependency upon the approval and acceptance of other; when they do not receive it, they get anxious, erratic, argumentative, sometimes to the point of anger when they are forced to be separated from their telephone or electronic device.

Gaining the approval of others is often enjoyable and can be a pathway towards multiple opportunities on a personal and professional level. But spending your energy on seeking approval also comes with a price, as we see above in our example. There isn't anything that is more detrimental to your *why* and that keeps you from being your authentic self then when we design our lives to appease others. The more we value the opinions of others, the less we value our own inherent worth. No matter what our society wants us to believe, our self-worth is something we decide for ourselves.

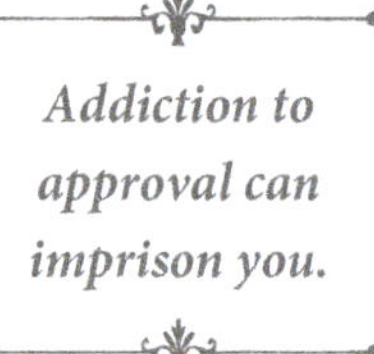

Addiction to approval can imprison you.

If you decide that your worth depends fully on how others perceive you; then you are addicted to approval. Moreover, by seeking someone else's validation, you are living a life that is not our own. Have you developed habits that are detrimental to your mental and physical health? Are you fearing rejection? This may look like listening to certain music, using illegal substances, and even supporting certain political or religious views just so you can gain the approval from a certain group of people. By doing this, you may become a part of a popular multitude, but you are exchanging it for your God-given gift of authenticity. Are you deceiving yourself? At the end of the day, an individual who lives an authentic life gains more respect than someone whose only goal is to appease others. Addiction to approval can imprison you.

You must craft your own identity!

You must be intentional about crafting your own identity. Otherwise, you will be relegated to a mediocre life in which others decide who you are and establish your personal *why's* for you. Don't allow it! Mediocrity is a place where your dreams and potential go to die! I promise that God has placed more in you than other people can imagine. Do not try to find the best of yourself through the approval of others. Self discovery is the key to identifying who you really are, and allowing the Holy Spirt to be your guide.

One thing affecting the world is the lack of people taking time to evaluate their *whys*. You may be spending more time doing than being! Some people get a job because they need to survive and mistreat customers because they don't enjoy what they do. Others rush into relationships because they want to fill the void of loneliness. When they get married, they realize that it did not solve the problem. As people continue making decisions without examining their *why*, the world we live in will continue to be contaminated by its ill effects. For example, some female teenagers grow up without a father, and the fruit of that malignant seed of abandonment is manifested through the feeling of rejection. Now they find themselves in situations where they want to water that seed. They begin to seek the love that they did not get from their father from others. Once the teenager gives into that desire, they may end up with an unwanted pregnancy, and that child ends up being raised by a single mother. It is sad to see these things continuously happening in the society.

The solution is to ask yourself some *why* questions. If you ask someone why they are in the relationship they are currently in, their response is because they love them. But, is that a good enough response to their *why*? Why do you love him? Why did you choose him? Once you answer these questions, you will know if the relationship is healthy. Examining your *why* is a valuable evaluating tool that is available to you whenever you need it. Use it and it just may spare you some heartache.

What does freedom have to do with it...everything!

Many people take life for granted and ignore the importance of freedom. Freedom is a state of exemption from the power or control of another. It is the ability to say *no* even when you want to say *yes*, because you know the consequences have the probability of ruining your life.

> *23 All things are lawful [a]for me, but not all things are helpful; all things are lawful for me, but not all things [b]edify. 24 Let no one seek his own, but each one the other's well-being.*
>
> **1 CORINTHIANS 10:23-26 (NKJV)**

You can do anything and everything you want, but not everything is good for you. Some of your actions may have the ability to damage yourself and others. When that happens, that is called a misuse of freedom. We live in a world where people are prone to believe that they have the freedom to do whatever they want without expecting any consequences whatsoever. Your freedom is meant to edify you and others by bringing unity and harmony to your community. Freedom is a gift we receive through Jesus Christ to enjoy and bring edification to the generations to come. If you are reading this book and don't know Jesus Christ as your Lord and Savior, I pray that you would accept Him today. (There is a Salvation Prayer at the end of the book.) By doing so, you will experience the real freedom that only comes through Him. Freedom gives you the ability to truly love yourself and others. Otherwise we may be on a path of self-destruction. When we refuse the light of God's love, we open the door to the destructive powers of Satan. Self-destruction is when you do things to harm yourself, whether emotional or physical. This person may constantly have suicidal thoughts and darkness blinds them, so they cannot see the goodness and beauty surrounding them.

In some cases, childhood trauma contributes to the initiation of self-destructive behaviors to the degree that they can sabotage personal and professional relationships. The person has no energy to engage fully in day-to-day life. They are on an assignment to destroy themselves no matter what. This is sad because they are completely out of focus. If you are experiencing this, you must make a deliberate attempt to stay focused on the journey to discover your purpose.

Destructive thoughts come from Satan. By accepting Jesus to be your Lord and Savior, the light of His truth comes in and exposes the plans of the enemy. You are fearlessly and wonderfully made! He does not want you to know that is who God designed you to be. People often get afraid when you mention making Jesus Christ your Lord and Savior, because they don't understanding what it means. When someone does not understand something, they tend to reject an idea without fully knowing its benefits, especially if it is not popular. The word *savior* means, *a person who rescues another from danger, and a person who helps others do what they can't do for themselves.* If you are struggling with something, Jesus can help you with it. It is through prayer that you communicate with Jesus regarding everything and anything. One of the things you can do through prayer is pray without limitations.

> *7 "Ask and it will be given to you; seek and you will find; knock and the door will be opened to you. 8 For everyone who asks receives; the one who seeks finds; and to the one who knocks, the door will be opened.*
> **MATTHEW 7:7-12 (NIV)**

A prayer posture puts you in the winning seat. Prayers have no geographical limitations, meaning they can go places that you can't. It is an important form of communication when you need divine intervention. Ask the Holy Spirit to help you align your *whys*. Once you receive the

The light illuminates the truth of what is inside you.

help and guidance, you will see things shift in a whole different direction, but it all starts with accepting Jesus Christ as your Lord and Savior.

Once you reevaluate your *why*, you will understand the reason behind the negativity in your life. This will help in so many ways and in so many areas. Through having a relationship with Jesus Christ, you can gain control over your life again. You are equipped to overcome all obstacles with the help of the Holy Spirit. You won't be able to do it alone because you need God's light to shine on the dark places in your life. The light illuminates the truth of what is inside you. When you bring truth into a place where only darkness has abided, it may feel uncomfortable, but this is only temporary. You will eventually enjoy this journey because it brings you closer to living an authentic and joyful life. By understanding the power of your *why*, you can also gain a greater ability to influence and help others.

So let's get busy discovering the real you!

It is time to sit and find out who the real you is?! Initially you will want to make a list of the positive and negative seeds (original thoughts) that you may have about yourself. Write then down on a piece of paper or an electronic page or notebook. Make two columns, and label one NEGATIVE, and the other POSITIVE. Once you are done put each description that is a negative such as: "I'm ugly. I'm good for nothing, other people seem to be smarter than me. I'm poor. My dad abandoned me, I'm a bastard," under that column. Now, write down all the positive thoughts, such as: "I'm beautiful. My mom loves me. I'm a good student, etc.," under the other column. As you continue writing, something amazing is going to occur; you will start recognizing that some of these seeds have been impacting your effectiveness in different areas. This is good because it means you are getting to know the true you. Bringing it to the table starts the process. Don't be afraid to dig deep inside; when you do, don't be afraid of what you find. Remember knowing the present status of your *why* has the power to revolutionize your life. With the help of the Holy Spirit, finding and facing your authentic self is one of the most powerful ways to find your true purpose!

CHAPTER 3

PLAN BREAKTHROUGH

He who is in you is greater than he who is in the world.
1 JOHN 4:4 (ESV)

People are often attracted to larger-than-life individuals, and that individual can be you! These are the words that continuously resonated in me as I entered the breakthrough process. A breakthrough means you have busted through every barrier and hindrance that has kept you from achieving the desires of your heart. You have completely destroyed Satan's attempts to steal, kill and destroy your life. That's something the world can't do. When you're pressed for a change—whether in your finances, health, or relationships—it is easy to look where everyone else does—to the world. The world offers a plethora of so-called "solutions." They often seem to be the door to a better life, but when you enter

Your breakthrough is inside you.

that door you realize that you were deceived by its seductive proposition. You often see this in advertisements that promote that there is a medicine for every symptom under the sun, a loan for every financial hardship, and a trendy relationship approach around every corner. But have you ever noticed that these quick fixes don't always work? At best, they put a bandage on the underlying issue that remains unaddressed and waiting to pop back up again. They don't get to the root. They don't provide what you desire most—*Breakthrough.*

If you have been looking to outside sources to fix your body, your marriage, or your finances, you are looking in the wrong place. *Your breakthrough is inside you.* Inside of you is a place where you will discover your truth and find the courage to live it on your own terms. Now, to do that, you must understand that you cannot do it without the light of the Lord. The light is important in your life to silence the confusion that exists in our environments; we must know the truth. The truth is found in the Word of God. The truth dwells in us through the Holy Spirit. The Holy Spirit is the person who Jesus Christ left as a counselor after his death and resurrection, to guide us through life as a believer. The Holy Spirit is the one that lights up a room for you to see what is inside. The light also reveals the small things that are hard to capture. He is the light that exposes all the things we need to work on that will eventually lead us to the breakthrough we desire. Many individuals desire a breakthrough, but don't desire the effervescent light of the Holy Spirit for the breakthrough. They believe that entering a room with a flashlight is enough to light up the room and wipe out their insecurities, self-imposed limitations, and fears. But my question would be, how? If you only have two hands and use one to hold the flashlight, you will become limited in what you can do.

Let's take a look at some of the challenges that might cause:

> A handheld flashlight is not designed to light up the entire room simultaneously.

> Holding a flashlight takes away from using the strength of both hands. Now let's put this in perspective. Let's say you need to carry a heavy box that clearly requires both your hands from dark room A to dark room B. How would you do it? You need to see, and you require both hands. That would become a nearly impossible task to accomplish.

> Due to the limited lighting, you can trip and fall.

> ➤ The flashlight is powered by a battery, which means that the flashlight's power is limited to the lifespan of the battery.

> ➤ The flashlight is controlled by an individual. The individual decides if he wants to use it or not.

Light is extremely important when you want to maneuver through a dark room full of things, especially if the room is messy. Many individuals have an interior mess, but they keep wanting to use a flashlight to illuminate it. We want a breakthrough but want to control the process. That will not work at all! That is why you need natural light, something like the sun, to light up everything to facilitate the cleaning process. This is what we call a breakthrough. As you can see, it is impossible to continue with the flashlight method to do a thorough job.

> [5] *Trust in the* LORD *with all your heart and lean not on your own understanding;*
>
> [6] *in all your ways submit to him, and he will make your paths straight.*[a]
>
> [7] *Do not be wise in your own eyes; fear the* LORD *and shun evil.*
>
> [8] *This will bring health to your body and nourishment to your bones.*
>
> **PROVERBS 3:5-8 (NIV)**

There are things in life that you believe you have control of, but in reality they have control over you. They have become your master without you even noticing it. You have entered into an agreement with it, and now you have become its slave. You are now addicted to what ever it is. How has this happened? Ask yourself, what happens when you are feeling depressed? Who or what do you run to? Who is your savior? Whatever you run to has now become your master. As children of God, you must run to your Heavenly Father daily through prayer, fasting, and meditating on his Word.

Unfortunately, we don't have to go far to see people who have become slaves to addiction. Just simply walking on the streets, you see addicts desperately seeking to survive. At some point in their lives, they thought they were in control until their appetite grew uncontrollable. Now the addiction places a yoke on their neck, controlling their every thought, word, and action. Many people believe that they have enough strength in themselves to control such things like anger, resentment, unforgiveness, violence, alcohol, traumas, drugs, prostitution, etc., not realizing that even though it seems easy to control, it is not. Don't be fooled by its temporary relief, eventually, it will grab ahold of you.

Your brain is a powerful supercomputer!

Your brain operates like a supercomputer and requires maintenance on a regular basis. The software needs to be updated, the battery protected, and the hard drive cleaned to operate at its maximum potential. The brain continuously moves and never stops because it seeks purpose. It is waiting for you to give it an assignment because it desperately desires to complete it. That's what it is designed to do. Some people want their mind to stop thinking because they are stressed. They are unable to control it. This keeps it from doing what it is designed to do. You have an amazing brain and you need to take care of it on a regular basis. Sometimes you may become fixated on your outward appearance, but also give some attention to your brain. You must renew it on a daily basis.

2 Do not conform to the pattern of this world, but be transformed by the renewing of your mind. Then you will be able to test and approve what God's will is—his good, pleasing and perfect will.

ROMANS 12:2 (NIV)

"We are called to be world changers, not world chasers."

- DR. CINDY TRIMM

What did Paul mean by "the renewal of your mind?" Simply put, renewing your mind is the process of exchanging lies for the truth. It is the exchange of your natural way of thinking for God's way of thinking. This means that renewing your mind is much more than knowing additional information or the power of positive thinking. There are some who think that the fundamental problem with the mind is that it does not have the knowledge it needs. Therefore, simply more education is the natural conclusion to the perceived problem. All you need is to "know more," and you will become a better person. Some people think the problem with the mind is dwelling too much on negative thoughts instead of positive ones, but the Bible has a deeper diagnosis. It teaches that you need more than new information; your mind itself needs to be renewed. You need more than the power of positive thinking; you need the power of God's way of thinking. Let's dig a little deeper.

In Ephesians 4:23, Paul says you must be "renewed in the spirit of your mind." Now, what is "the spirit of your mind?" It is the power or governing principle of your mind. Think of it this way – the human mind is like a movie theater. It does not just have a screen of random images and thoughts; it has a projector that is set to run particular thoughts and images on that screen. This is what some call your "mindset," and because of the fall, the human mind is set up to project lies instead of truth, and false images instead of true images. This is the fundamental problem of the mind that needs to change through the "renewal of the Holy Spirit" (Titus 3:5). Therefore, the Bible speaks of the mind needing to be set "on the things above" (Colossians.3:2) or "set on the things of the Spirit" (Romans.8:5). Lasting change must start with in the mindset that directs what images or thoughts the mind projects.

This is not an optional step during the process of change; it is an essential step. Mind-renewal is necessary to make any progress in the Christian life. Think of it this way – no mind change, no life change. Our manner of life is directly linked to the life of our mind. Your particular mindset about God, other people, yourself, situations, things, the future, etc., directly influences how you will feel, speak, and act. For example, the reason you may live for money or human approval is because of a lie that you believe about what money, or the praise of people will bring you. The reason you may live in despair is because of a lie that you believe about your past, present or future. For that reason, it is important to renew your mind. Therefore, we should look at our minds as a supercomputer. We must pay attention to things in our daily routine or habits that contribute to how we are downloading information into our brain. The how is just as important as the why!

The brain can obtain and absorb so much more information than we can imagine. As we look at the health of the brain, we realize that it is a living mechanism that also needs care. Anything that is alive will demand care. Let us look at the updated software that your brain needs. Some of the ways you can update your software is by reading books, which is why you are currently reading this book. You are reading this book because you are updating your software through the revelation that the Lord has brought through this book. It is important that we update our system not only through books but through other means like podcasts or life experiences. When we go through a

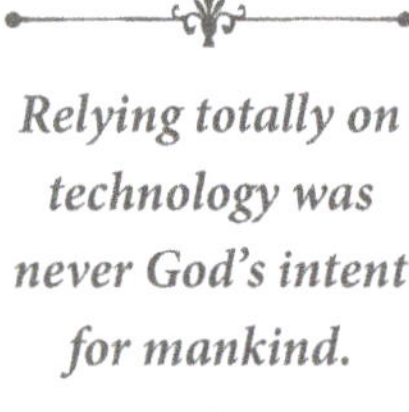

crisis, it can get the worst, or best out of you. The crisis can either break you or make you. I believe that a crisis has the potential to cause you to manifest the best creative and divine ideas; form world changing solutions internally, and be birthed out into this world for others to benefit. A crisis is a sign that you must dig deep into yourself to find the solution for that situation. The problem is that individuals don't realize that if you don't choose what to feed your brain with, the brain will choose it automatically. The reason it does it automatically is because it was created to do so. Information passes through the door of the eyes, captures everything, and then gives it form. If you constantly watch a movie about anger and violence, your brain will tell your body to mimic what it saw. The brain will continue reminding the body of what they saw until it is manifested into flesh. That is why many people fall into depression or anxiety because they keep allowing the system of this world to feed them, instead of taking full authority and control over what they want to upgrade their systems with. Upgrading your system is a daily routine necessary to grow your brain. You can expand your comprehension in any field you desire to master by feeding your brain information about that specific industry.

Relying totally on technology was never God's intent for mankind. Unfortunately, we are allowing some of these technological advancements influence the upgrading of our personal supercomputer to the point of disabling us. Some companies are working on creating human-like robots to substitute humans. Why? God has gifted us with a supercomputer called the brain. He has placed his characteristics in us and given us free will, which the world wants to remove from us. That is why it is crucial that you upgrade your system by reading the bible and other educational books that will expand your growth to become an asset to this world and not a liability. The importance of upgrading is that you become a solution to this world and not another problem. The people perish for lack of knowledge. Now we have audible books, which are like listening to a bedtime story. You don't have to hold the book in your hands anymore; you just sit back, relax, listen, and meditate. We have technology that we can use for us and not against us. We need to get closer to the truth of who we are and who God is. We must get closer to knowing and understanding the times we are living in. The world is confused; it is in crisis. Many people have lost their identity and the power of their original purpose.

Recharging your brain

The way you strategically prepare for a breakthrough is by protecting the battery that energizes your brain. We must make having time to rest and recharge a priority. Some of us have a bad habit of going to sleep late and waking up early, which may produce mental fatigue or tiredness and make our brains lethargic. Have you ever experienced not being well rested? A typical side effect is becoming sensitive and explosive to anything and everything. This adversely affects your performance.

Another way you can protect your brain's battery is by connecting with nature. In the bible, we read a story about Adam and Eve and how they were in the garden and nourished themselves with the food that nature provided. We see that in the garden, there were vegetables, fruits, and natural food that would benefit the body. In the garden, Adam had dominion over everything, and was able to give his body what it needed. There are natural foods that you can eat to strengthen your brain's cells.

A brain that is able to come up with solutions is considered healthy. If you watch movies that have negative morals and attitudes, you will start adopting unhealthy strategies to deal with situations that arise. This could lead to a heart filled with bitterness instead of compassion as intended by God. This negative outlook could turn people away and hinder your potential to become a wise, powerful and thoughtful leader. There are many corrupted leaders in the world, and we witness their actions and consequences every day. Proverbs 29:2 (KJV) states that when righteous people rule, the people rejoice, but when wicked people rule, the people mourn. It is important that righteous people are in charge. If you are a leader, it is important to prioritize a healthy brain. Remember that you need to have the mind of Christ to do righteous work on earth.

You can also strengthen your brain through a technology detox. It is important to disconnect from watching social media, which can sidetrack you from having a healthy brain. By continuing to feed your brain the food of social media, you will start to feel drained and confused because you started departing from who you are for something that you are not. Lies have deceived numerous people and placed them in a cave of darkness. Many people have allowed social media to define their identity instead of leading them to self-discovery. Imagine living a life like an imposter and cheating the world by not living in the authenticity of yourself. The authentic you can restore others. They will see your smile, and your smile will bring healing to their soul. They will hear your voice, and the wise council will set them free from financial struggles.

Discovering yourself is the most beautiful journey anyone can ever go on. As I went into my journey of self-discovery, I learned so much about myself and explored my capacities and abilities regarding problem-solving. The inner journey is the best place to go for a mental staycation. It can be compared to visiting beautiful places that are memorable and life changing.

As you continue this journey of your breakthrough, it is important that you clean your computer's hard drive, which are your memories. The way you clean the hard drive of the brain is through meditation, journaling, and prayer. It is important that you take time to meditate on where you have been, where you are, and where you are heading. This is a crucial moment because that will help you reduce the clutter of tasks that you erroneously committed to along the way. So establishing your *why* again is important to this process.

The Need for Self-Discipline

> [23] *I do all this for the sake of the gospel, that I may share in its blessings.* [24] *Do you not know that in a race all the runners run, but only one gets the prize? Run in such a way as to get the prize.* [25] *Everyone who competes in the games goes into strict training. They do it to get a crown that will not last, but we do it to get a crown that will last forever.*

1 CORINTHIANS 9:23-25 (NIV)

Self discipline is the key to staying focused and staying in the race. The by-product of a healthy mind is the ability to live prosperously in all areas of life. Discipline is the training or developing through instruction and exercise the fruit of self-control. Discipline *provides people with the parameters to live their lives efficiently and effectively*. When you have discipline in your life, you can make small sacrifices in the present for a better life in the future. Discipline creates habits, habits make routines, and routines become who you are daily. That is why discipline and focus are important, especially for your brain's health.

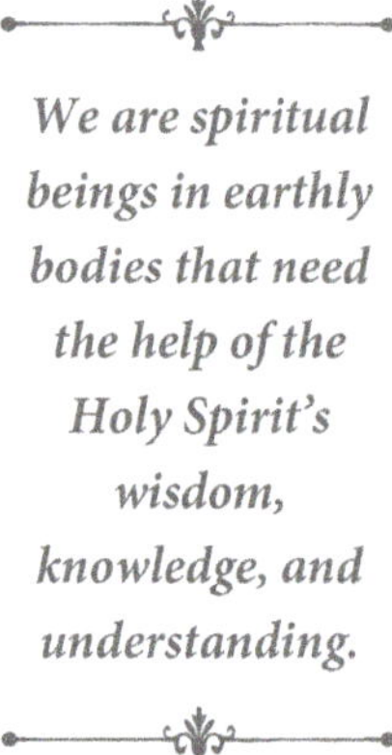

We are spiritual beings in earthly bodies that need the help of the Holy Spirit's wisdom, knowledge, and understanding.

Journaling energizes the brain. It brings clarity and makes room for self-evaluation. It is important that you put what's in your brain on paper. As you write, you will start making space for new and updated information. Be selective about what new and updated information you feed into your brain. You can input updated poor, unhealthy and corrupted information, or on the other hand, edifying, healthy, constructive information. It is crucial when deciding what information to upgrade because that information may produce unwanted fruits. That is why it is very important that you have submitted to the Holy Spirit and regained control of your thoughts. Your daily disciplines determines where you are heading.

As you journal, it is important to read the bible, meditate on what you read and pray about it. When you read the bible, God will speak the truth to you and help you with your daily responsibilities. The helper, the Holy Spirit, will impart the truth of life in your mind, bringing health to your body, mind, and spirit. We are spiritual beings in earthly bodies that need the help of the Holy Spirit's wisdom, knowledge, and understanding. To obtain that, we must keep in mind to fear the Lord. Fearing the Lord means respect and reverence; giving Him the attention He deserves.

We, as human beings, can be very challenging to deal with. We demand so much from everyone except ourselves. We demand others to respect and listen to us, but we are challenged when it is required of us. We demand resources, but don't want to put in the work, time, education, patience, compassion, or build the understanding to garner them. We demand from others what we should be demanding from ourselves. There are times when we start demanding God to do some things for us, when he is waiting for us to do it. Some people get upset with God because he did not do what they demanded him to do. Those individuals attempt to discredit God's existence because of their personal failure. When you hear people discrediting God, it is simply because they placed a demand on God without realizing that God was waiting on them the whole time, and He still is. It is sad to hear people speaking about God in such ignorance because they never took the time to get to know his heart through meditating on his word, journaling, and praying. To hear God, you must want Him, listen for Him, and look for Him. According to 1 Chronicles 28:9 and 2 Chronicles 15:2, *if you seek Him, He will be found by you.*

The easiest place to find Him is in the Bible. Read the Bible for fun, believing it really happened. Ask God what is He trying to say to you when you read. Ask Him what He wants to show you, then stop talking and listen. Be attentive and listen until you hear Him. In addition to the Bible, God can talk to you in any way He wants. That doesn't mean it is easy to always hear Him. Many things can block your hearing from God:

entertainment distractions, time constraints, traditions, and erroneous doctrines. The enemy will try to find ways to fight against you, but if you seek God, He will be found by you. God's methods easily trumps any card the enemy has. God does not force Himself on you; keep that in mind. So, just continue to look for Him, listen to Him, and then act on what He has said. When you obey Him, it helps you understand His ways, and helps you hear Him better the next time you listen for a word from Him.

As you prepare for your breakthrough, it is important that you sit and meditate on everything you have just read. Start seeking books to update your software (way of thinking) regarding the truth of who you are. You must schedule "me moments," where you put everything aside and focus on God alone. This is a time that you separate yourself from the whole world, and you abide in the presence of Almighty God, getting to know His truth for your life. He is ready willing and able to share life changing revelations with you. Make the connection with the help of the Holy Spirit!

CHAPTER 4

DETOXIFICATION

As life happens, you may fail to realize how much your soul has been contaminated by circumstances in life. It is crazy to see how much time and energy we use to survive. Often times we ignore the need to detoxify the lies that have been planted in us. We need to change them into the truth. Many of you have been living contaminated lives because of the corrupt system of this world. The system of this world uses different institutional norms to contaminate you. These things have distorted your clarity about what you really should be doing. This contamination can blur your vision, forcing you to walk in mediocracy. You need to be detoxified!

> *"Therefore, if anyone cleanses himself from these things, he will be a vessel for honor, sanctified, useful to the Master, prepared for every good work."*
>
> **2 TIMOTHY 2:21 (NIV)**

It is extremely important that we understand our soul is the source of what makes us alive.

> *²³ Keep your heart with all diligence, For out of it spring the issues of life.*
>
> **PROVERBS 4:23 (NKJV)**

Human beings are not just bodies, but souls in bodies. To be more accurate, we are souls who interact with the physical world through our physical bodies. We are also souls who interact with the spiritual world. Though science has yet to discover a way to determine where our physical bodies end and where our souls begin, we are still more soul than body. One day our bodies will pass away and return to dust, but our souls will go on into eternity. Your soul is the source of your healing, purpose, and personal success. When it has been seeded by the Spirit of Christ and watered by the word of God, you flourish.

How did you get to where you are today?

Where you are today is based on the decisions you made yesterday. I heard someone describe it this way; the day you were born, you were given two proverbial envelopes. On the front of one was written "pleasure, faith and prosperity," on the other envelope was written "pain, fear, and disease." When each envelope was opened, they contained the same pages labeled "destiny." You get to choose your destiny.

God has given you the power to be a decision-maker to change circumstances and reverse negative human conditions. As an individual, you must be intentional about the kind of changes you want to make in your life, your home, your community, your ministry, your business, your government, your school, your health care system, and your nation.

When your soul prospers, you prosper.

As we enter this journey of detoxification of the soul, we must understand that we need the help of our Lord Jesus Christ. We must let Jesus sit on the throne of our hearts and submit our will, emotions, and everything to Him. When initiating this procedure, it is important to know the following:

> *² Beloved, I pray that all may go well with you and that you may be in good health, as it goes well with your soul.*
>
> **3 JOHN 2 (ESV)**

One of the things this passage is telling us is that as your soul prospers, everything else will prosper. This reinforces the importance of taking time to examine what is in the soul. Some of us want to be prosperous, but ignore the soul when the soul is the primary place where you should seek to prosper. Prosperity is moving forward, achieving accomplishments, success, advancement and thriving. It is also when you experience the fullness of the blessing of God. Now, in order to get to that realm of prosperity, you must ask the Holy Spirit for His assistance.

The key to living a blessed life is cleansing the soul. Many people have lived with such remorse, hatred, anger, and lack of forgiveness in their souls that it weakens their health, wealth, and power. They go through life experiencing sickness and having multiple health issues. Doctors seem to have no explanation for the symptoms. There is a possibility that some of your health issues are associated with soul issues. In the bible, there was a man named Saul, who God chose to be the King of Israel. As time passed, God told the Prophet Samuel to give Saul instructions on what to do with the land and the people of Amalec. He told him that because Amalec sought to destroy Israel. He was instructed to kill everyone and not leave anyone alive. Once Saul and his army went to attack the Amalecs, he noticed that they had great wealth. So he kept the wealth and the King from that region alive. The Prophet Samuel was upset at Saul for being disobedient. Due to his disobedience and unrepentant heart, the bible says that evil spirits started tormenting him. Imagine that God gives you instructions, and you are only partially obedient, meaning you were disobedient. Once Saul was being tormented, he could not sleep; he had insomnia. The only way he was able to rest was when David's worship of the Lord soothed his soul. Saul would call David to play the harp so he could rest and sleep in peace. Many are currently suffering from lack of sleep due to their ongoing thoughts of anxiety, worries, insecurities, or other things that have stolen their peace. In their soul, there may be a lack of forgiveness, anger, resentment, bitterness, and other things that do not allow them to live an abundant life in Jesus Christ.

In this world, our soul, which is our will, mind, and emotions, has been contaminated with digital media, life experiences, and unpredictable circumstances. It is time to detox the soul. It is important to always have a system in place for a healthy mentality. Why? Because we must examine our soul for any contamination that it might have picked up. If we do not have a system in place for the cleansing, our perspective of life starts to shift into destructive thinking.

According to the National Science Foundation, 80% of the thoughts we think are negative and 95% of our thoughts are repetitive. Some people believe they are experts in hiding the things that are in their souls, not knowing that everything has a language. For example, the language of emotional pain can be expressed when an individual is continuously seeking isolation or separation from the people they love. It can also be expressed through words of guilt, helplessness, or hopelessness. Have you ever heard someone speak about life as if everyone and everything is against them? They believe they are not worthy of anything good happening to them. The challenging part of this situation is that the individual can't detect the pain in their soul because they are used to the language connected with the emotional pain. Another sign that reveals emotional suffering is poor self-care, agitated anger, or moodiness. Hurting people hurt people. We live in a broken world, and only through the Holy Spirit can we live a life of unbrokenness, joy, peace, and abundance. Knowing that you can live a greater and more authentic life filled with authority and dominion is powerful.

Now let's get back to detoxifying your soul!

To proceed with the cleansing of the soul, it is important that you take the first step by acknowledging what is in the soul that needs to be dealt with. Acknowledgement means to accept, recognize, confirm, or admit the existence or truth of something. You must ask the Holy Spirit to navigate in your soul and enlighten you on what is in there that needs to be healed and accept that it is there. You would not intentionally eat or drink a poison that could harm or destroy your body. Yet, you may be consuming poison that is hazardous to your soul without even realizing it. Toxic attitudes, behaviors, and cultural influences that you allow into your life may put your soul in danger. You cannot avoid contact with such toxins in this fallen world, but you don't have to remain contaminated by them.

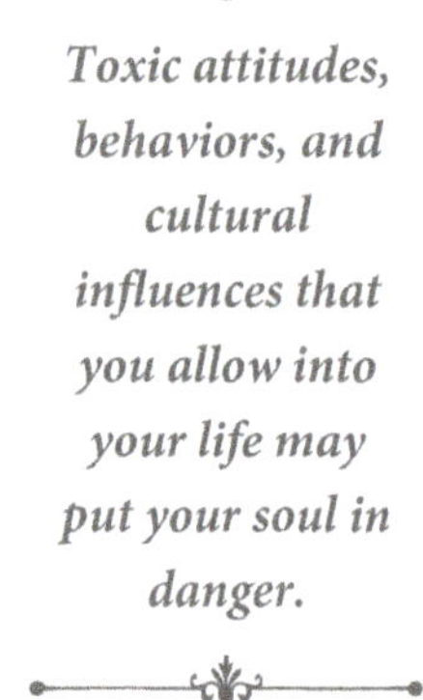

Toxic attitudes, behaviors, and cultural influences that you allow into your life may put your soul in danger.

You can detoxify your soul and start experiencing the pure life that God wants you to enjoy. It is important to realize that everything counts. Absolutely everything that you allow into your mind and life has an impact on how you grow or don't grow spiritually.

The little choices that you make every day have a significant effect on your soul. So, take your everyday decisions seriously. Examine your life for: toxic behaviors (what you do that harms your spiritual effectiveness or distracts you from God's purposes for your life), emotions (feelings that lead you away from God's truth), and consumptions (media you consume and people you spend time with). Ask God to give you the wisdom you need to discern which of all these things are toxic to you. Clean up your thoughts. Since spiritual battles are ultimately either won or lost in the mind, it's crucial to pay attention to what thoughts you focus on. Your thoughts shape what kind of person you become. If you think unhealthy thoughts, you will become an unhealthy person. But if you think healthy thoughts that reflect God's truth, you will become more like Jesus, as God intends you to become. Regularly pray for the ability to view the situations you encounter as God sees them so you can have the right perspective. Every day, ask God to show you which thoughts that enter your mind are unholy and displeasing to Him. Whenever you identify wrong thoughts, take action to replace them with the right ones. Choose to focus only on thoughts about what is true, noble, right, pure, lovely, admirable, excellent, or praiseworthy. Spend time meditating on God's wonderful qualities; the more you think about God, the more peace will enter your mind. The other area you need to consider is breaking free of fear. Whenever you feel afraid, remind yourself that fear never comes from God; it comes from the evil one. God gives you a spirit of power, love, and peace – not fear. Rather than placing your faith in all the "what-ifs" of life and feeling afraid of what may or may not happen, place your faith in God, who is in charge of your future and wants what's best for you. Pay attention to specific, persistent fears in your life because they reveal the areas in which you are trusting God the least. Pray about each area you identify as a problem, surrendering each one specifically to God and asking Him to help you trust Him more with it. Then be diligent about seeking God so you can consistently grow closer to Him. The closer you become to God, the less you will struggle with fear.

Once you overcome fear, you can now dig up the bitter roots from your soul. When you allow bitterness to take root in your soul, it poisons you and blocks you from experiencing the grace God wants to give you. So, let's get rid of bitterness by following God's command to forgive people who have hurt you. Bitterness is usually associated with being angry and holding grudges. It is a negative emotion or attitude negatively affected by a bad experience. It is feeling anger and disappointment about being treated unfairly and harboring resentment. Hurt leads to bitterness.

One of the ways to root out bitterness is through forgiveness. Forgiveness is a God-given gift that you give to those who have offended you or harmed you. For most of us, that's easier said than done. Only through God's grace can you truly forgive others and yourself. It was by God's grace that all your sins are forgiven. It was his grace that brought restoration to your soul. You can forgive others for the hurt they have caused you because God's grace flows through you. Sometimes, the most difficult person to forgive is yourself. To truly forgive yourself, you need God's grace. Only His grace can empower you to forgive your past mistakes and sins. How can you not forgive yourself when God has already forgiven you? As you show others the same grace and forgiveness Christ gives you, the roots of bitterness inside you will wither and die. It takes time, but as you release forgiveness through God's grace, you will find new freedom, joy, and happiness.

See to it that no one comes short of the grace of God; that no root of bitterness springing up causes trouble, and by it many be defiled.

HEBREWS 12:15 (NIV)

Make these confessions.

- ➢ With God's grace – I will not allow bitterness to take hold of me.
- ➢ With God's grace – I forgive others the way Christ forgives me.
- ➢ With God's grace – I forgive myself of my past sins and mistakes.
- ➢ With God's grace – I'm pulling up every root of bitterness growing in my heart.

In Jesus 'Name, Amen.

You must pay close attention to what's going on in your life to get rid of the toxic influences. Break free of materialism and look to God (instead of money and possessions) to meet your needs for happiness, significance, and security. Whenever you consume media of any kind (from television shows, songs, Internet articles, and books), honestly ask yourself: "Am I being entertained by sin?" "Is this pleasing to God?"" "Does this lure me away from Jesus?" If the answer is *yes*, stop consuming the media that you recognize is toxic. Since bad company corrupts good character, set boundaries to protect yourself from being influenced by unhealthy people, and cut off unhealthy relationships with people who are dangerous to your spiritual growth. It is important that you recognize who these people are because if you don't, you will feel weak and then question where the negative pull is coming from. Sometimes it is uncomfortable to let go of people you have been with for a long time, but it is necessary. Once you get rid of those people, you are ready for the new influencers that will push you to the next level. Some people have influenced you without you realizing it is happening; that's what I call the invisible influencers. The invisible influencers are those things that you do without noticing you are doing them. That is why you must ask God to show you when the spirit of religion is corrupting the purity of the Gospel in your life, and to help you focus not on using your external behavior to earn God's love, but on responding to the love that God has already given you by trusting Him in all ways.

"Don't let anyone rent a space in your head unless they are a good tenant."

\- GEORGE COUROS

Affirmations to help you ignore toxic people:

1. When I hear something negative, I will replace it with a positive.

2. I have control of my emotions.

3. My success depends on staying focused.

4. I accept the fact that I cannot change people, but I can change myself.

5. I am powerful, and no one can take it from me.

6. I will not give in to the negativity of toxic people.

7. I am happy and positive no matter who is around me.

8. I am using the situation as a learning opportunity for what I don't want to be.

9. I am not letting toxic people get me down.

10. I will let go of people who don't support me and don't care about me.

11. I know my worth, and I recognize my value.

12. I can choose the people I want in my life.

13. The less I respond to negative people, the more peaceful my life is.

14. This day belongs to me.

15. I willingly edit my life and its content.

16. I take responsibility for a joyful and peaceful life.

These affirmations will help you see that you are in control and optimizing your ability to live a consecrated life, devoted to Christ. Repeat them daily with the understanding that God has set you free, and through him, you are an overcomer in any and every area of your life. You can do all things through Christ who strengthens you. I want to encourage you to keep trying even if you don't succeed, dust yourself off, and try again. Jesus' victory over darkness has given you the keys to living a better and greater life.

Now let us look at your spirit!

A strong spirit is a major key to a productive life in the Kingdom of God. As a Christian, your spiritual condition will determine your life's quality. If a person gets born-again and makes Jesus the Lord of their life, but fails to develop and maintain their spiritual growth continuously, they will fall short of everything that God has called them to do. Therefore, as believers, it is imperative that we do everything necessary to make sure that we are strong.

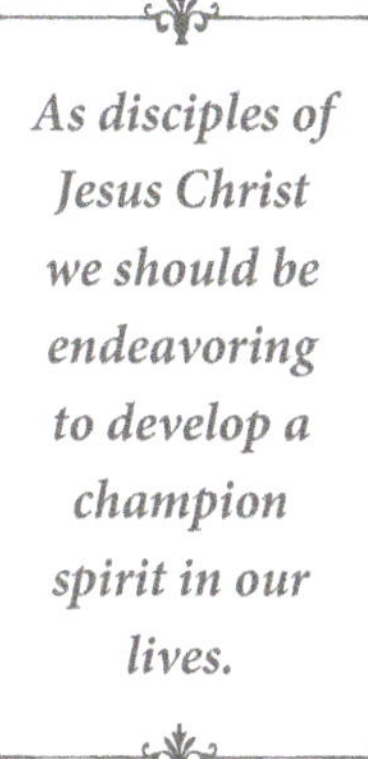

As disciples of Jesus Christ we should be endeavoring to develop a champion spirit in our lives.

As disciples of Jesus Christ we should be endeavoring to develop a *champion spirit* in our lives. A champion is one who wins, one who fights, one who has defeated and surpassed all rivals, one who is superior and has all the attributes of a winner. You should be fighting the good fight of faith and experiencing victory over the adversary by exercising your spiritual muscles. Our spirits should be superior to our minds and bodies rather than being controlled by them. They should possess all the attributes of a winner. Our spirits should perfectly embody all that Jesus was when He walked the Earth and all that He still is today. This is a *champion spirit*, and the first step to becoming a champion is detoxifying your soul.

As you experience these changes and see the outcome, you will realize that it is all worth it. Psalm 51:1 (NIV) says,

> *Have mercy on me, O God, according to your unfailing love; according to your great compassion blot out my transgressions. Wash away all my iniquity and cleanse me from my sin.*

There is nothing better than doing the possible and the Holy Spirit doing the impossible. You cannot expect God to work in your understanding of the realm of possibilities; he works in a limitless capacity.. When God cleanses you, you will see the fruits of the spirit that will operate in your life in such a way that people will want the fruit you are carrying. The fruits are a representation of the results you cultivated with the help of the Holy Spirit. Keep working with the help of the Holy Spirit to obtain divine results that will bring changes to a confused world. It's imperative that you continuously examine your fruit because the quality of your harvest depends on the seed sown, the soil it's planted in, and the threshing floor where it is harvested.

CHAPTER 5

APPLICATION

But be doers of the word, and not hearers only, deceiving yourselves.
JAMES 1:22 (NIV)

The title demands action. The verse above gives you instructions that will lead you to live a life with purpose. Many of us know that it is not enough to just have the knowledge of something because knowledge without application is a waste of information. Information has an assignment: to shed light on the knowledge that will take you to the next level. Information should not be taken lightly, especially if it will help you grow. The next step to continue the journey of growing into your purpose is understanding the power that exists behind doing something. The Bible says that faith without works is not faith. Faith is the ability to move with conviction towards something that has not yet been manifested in an individual's life. For example, when God is working with you, he teaches you through his word that the father of lies is Satan and there are consequences when you follow his lead. Once you receive that information through the scriptures, you meditate on it and it becomes knowledge, ready for application. Once the word is ready for application, wisdom comes in place to apply the word, and through the application, you display the glory of God.

Another example is when God is teaching you to forgive others the same way he has forgiven you. When you receive the information and meditate on it, then it becomes knowledge and is ready for action. When you read the word of God and it renews your mind, the knowledge of what you have received can liberate you to accomplish what's needed. In this case it is being able to

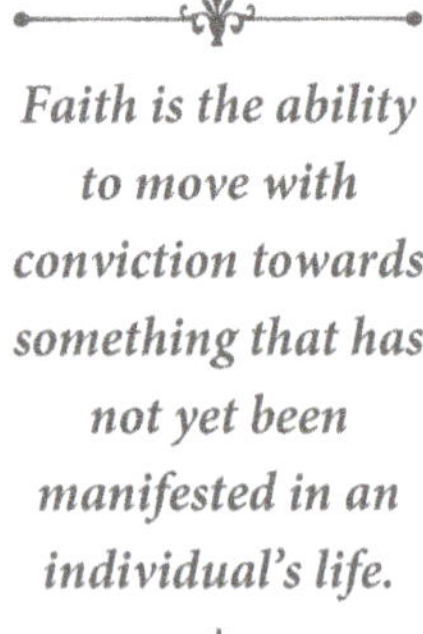

forgive someone. So, now you have received the gift of forgiving those that have hurt you. Forgiveness is a gift that is received through a relationship established with the Holy Spirit through prayer.

When seeking to discover our purpose in a world full of confusion, the Holy Spirit plays a crucial role. While many of us may turn to self-help books and other resources for guidance, the Bible holds a unique power. Through the help of the Holy Spirit, the word of God can transform individuals and prepare them to bear fruit that benefits themselves and those around them. However, the process of applying this knowledge can be challenging, especially when facing personal habits, pride, rejection, and defense mechanisms built up over time. Despite these obstacles, reading Ephesians 1:7 and realizing the love, redemption, and value we have in God can be a powerful tool for transformation.

I often wondered why God would choose someone like me, who struggles with learning and retention, comes from a dysfunctional family, and has been disowned by her father for being a girl. I questioned what God saw in me that warranted his attention. However, I found solace in a story from the Bible about David, who was rejected by his father and brothers but was anointed by God to be the King of Israel. This story resonated with me, as I too often felt burdened with more responsibilities than my brothers due to being the only girl in the family. Although I didn't understand it at the time, I now realize that these challenges were necessary for my growth and development. In life, God uses difficult situations to train us and prepare us for what is to come.

During my journey of self-discovery, I gained a better understanding of myself in relation to God and who He is. Through the story of David, I learned that even if one faces rejection and difficult training, it is important to persevere as these experiences build necessary skills for the future. The Holy Spirit is eager for us to practice and live out the teachings of God. By doing so, we become a testament to His glory. Thus, it is crucial to read and understand the word of God, allowing it to permeate our entire being and enable Him to work in our lives. As we listen to His guidance, we can discover our purpose and destiny. Devoting time each day to practice and apply the teachings of God can lead to personal growth and transformation.

Here are some potential barriers to accomplishing your purpose.

As you read the word of God, you will see some of the areas in your life that need shifting. You will need to ask the Holy Spirit to examine your soul, and identify the following things that you may have have held on to for too long:

- Lack of forgiveness
- Rejections
- Identity Thief
- Abandonments
- Disappointments
- Anger/Hot Temper
- Loneliness
- Deceptions
- Self-condemnation
- Guilt
- Self-resentment
- Fear of failure
- Suicide
- Self -Pity
- and many more…

Once you have identified what needs to be renounced, it is important to individually address each issue that the Holy Spirit brings to your attention. This requires attentive focus and utilizing the inner light to begin the application process. The first step is to acknowledge the issue and then proceed with renouncing it. This process may evoke strong emotions like crying or yelling, but it is a necessary part of the journey. The Comforter is there to provide support and guide you through the transformation. Any pain experienced during this process is a sign of weakness leaving your soul. Trust in God to lead the transformation in the way that is best for you. It is important to not allow anything or anyone to interfere with the process. This process is similar to the creation of heaven and earth in the Book of Genesis 1, and it can reveal things about yourself that you never knew existed. When someone goes through a transformation process and discovers their purpose, it is crucial to combine prayer and fasting with the word of God.

Below are some verses that you can declare and apply to your life to start seeing transformation. Just remember to be patient with yourself as you transform into the new you.

Forgiving Others

When we forgive others, we outwit Satan.

> [10] *If you forgive someone, then I also forgive them. And what I have forgiven—if I had anything to forgive—I forgave it for you, and Christ was with me.* [11] *I did this so that Satan would not win anything from us. We know very well what his plans are.*

2 CORINTHIANS 2:10-11 (ERV)

Forgiving others is not an option: it is a commandment of the Scripture.

> *¹² God has chosen you and made you his holy people. He loves you. So your new life should be like this: Show mercy to others. Be kind, humble, gentle, and patient. ¹³ Don't be angry with each other, but forgive each other. If you feel someone has wronged you, forgive them. Forgive others because the Lord forgave you.*

COLOSSIANS 3:12-13 (ERV)

Practical Steps:

> ➢ Seek guidance from God to identify individuals in your life that require your forgiveness. Create a record of their names and reasons for your resentment towards them, and store it in a balloon. Releasing the balloon signifies letting go of any bitterness you hold. As you release the balloon, repeat the phrase, "I forgive them," and continue to affirm your forgiveness towards them and their actions.

> ➢ Read Genesis 50:19-21. How did Joseph forgive?

Rejection

The great exchange was executed; He was rejected so that we might be accepted.

> *⁶ to the praise of the glory of His grace, by which He [a]made us accepted in the Beloved.*

EPHESIANS 1:6 (NKJV)

There is no rest in rejection. Rejection torments.

¹³ For you created my inmost being; you knit me together in my mother's womb.

PSALM 139:13 (NIV)

Practical Steps:

> ➤ Declare the following: "I am who Jesus wants me to be, and I am here because He wants me here. I am not a MISTAKE. Jesus makes no mistakes, and I will choose what Jesus wants for me, even if it goes against my own feelings or emotions."

> ➤ Declare Jeremiah 1:5, *You chose me before you gave me life. Before I was born, you selected me to be a voice to the people and to the nations.*

Anger/Hot Temper

Control yourself.

²⁸ Like a city whose walls are broken through is a person who lacks self-control.

PROVERBS 25:28 (NIV)

Avoiding anger requires listening, talking less, proceeding slowly, and not overreacting.

⁹ Do not be quickly provoked in your spirit, for anger resides in the lap of fools.

ECCLESIASTES 7:9 (NIV)

Practical Steps:

> ➤ Remember the things that cause you to get angry. What prompted it? What were your feelings and thoughts? Use this to identify and avoid your triggers.

> ➤ Memorize Ecclesiastes 7:9. When you sense anger coming, ask yourself if you are being a fool.

Disappointments

God knows and cares about our broken hearts.

> *15 For this is what the high and exalted One says—he who lives forever, whose name is holy: 'I live in a high and holy place, but also with the one who is contrite and lowly in spirit, to revive the spirit of the lowly and to revive the heart of the contrite.*
>
> **ISAIAH 57:15 (NIV)**

God will respond to our needs. Relief is coming.

> *18 The LORD is close to the brokenhearted and saves those who are crushed in spirit.*
>
> **PSALM 34:18 (NIV)**

Practical Steps:

> ➤ Write out and compare your negative responses to disappointment. Make a list of positive responses to that counteract your negative responses. Which will you choose?

> ➤ Memorize Psalm 34:18. Dwell on the fact that God will never disappoint you. Know That your Creator is absolutely faithful!

Loneliness

Paul's solution to loneliness.

> *"16 At my first defense, no one came to my support, but everyone deserted me. May it not be held against them. 17 But the Lord stood at my side and gave me strength, so that through me the message might be fully proclaimed and all the Gentiles might hear it. And I was delivered from the lion's mouth. 18 The Lord will rescue me from every evil attack and will bring me safely to his heavenly kingdom. To him be glory for ever and ever. Amen."*
>
> **2 TIMOTHY 4:16-18 (NIV)**

➢ God provided for Elijah's needs when he felt alone.

➢ We are not ever alone, because of the availability of the Holy Spirit.

> *5 A father to the fatherless, a defender of widows, is God in his holy dwelling. 6 God sets the lonely in families,[a] he leads out the prisoners with singing; but the rebellious live in a sun-scorched land.*
>
> **PSALM 68:5-6 (NIV)**

Practical Steps:

➢ Find opportunities for volunteer service in your church or community. Get out and help others!

➢ Use a journal to write yourself encouraging notes. Read through the Psalms and write the verses that bring comfort when someone is experiencing loneliness.

Suicide

There is no problem too difficult for God to handle.

> *¹⁷ "Ah, Sovereign LORD, you have made the heavens and the earth by your great power and outstretched arm. Nothing is too hard for you.*
>
> **JEREMIAH 32:17 (NIV)**

God will never leave us.

> *⁸ The LORD himself goes before you and will be with you; he will never leave you nor forsake you. Do not be afraid; do not be discouraged."*
>
> **DEUTERONOMY 31:8 (NIV)**

Practical Steps:

> ➢ Seek to help others as a sign of gratitude for God's love.
>
> ➢ Make a list of the Ten Commandments and identify which one you need to work on as a sign of love and respect towards God.

Trust/Faith

Trusting God shows confidence that his timing is perfect.

> *³ For the revelation awaits an appointed time; it speaks of the end and will not prove false. Though it linger, wait for it; it[a] will certainly come and will not delay. ⁴ "See, the enemy is puffed up; his desires are not upright—but the righteous person will live by his faithfulness[b]*
>
> **HABAKKUK 2:3-4 (NIV)**

The results from trusting God:

- ➢ Protection - Psalm 5:11
- ➢ Gladness - Psalm 64:10
- ➢ Peace - Isaiah 26:3-4
- ➢ Blessing - Psalm 84:12
- ➢ Confidence - Psalm 112:7

It is important to maintain trust in God and utilize the resources He has given you during this journey in order to attain success. Proper utilization of these resources may lead to a significant personal transformation, and gratitude towards God should be expressed for His guidance throughout this transformational journey.

CHAPTER 6

HARVEST TIME - THE RESULT

These have come so that the proven genuineness of your faith—of greater worth than gold, which perishes even though refined by fire— may result in praise, glory and honor when Jesus Christ is revealed.

1 Peter 1:7 (NIV)

The beauty of life is that you can always expect to receive a harvest after sowing seed. In this case, you have been investing time in your transformation journey. I know you have started to see a difference in some areas of your life. I guarantee that the way you think is shifting, and the way you see life, situations, or circumstances are changing. You are no longer a slave of the system of this world, but now you have been transferred from the kingdom of darkness to the kingdom of light, from the kingdom of ignorance to the kingdom of divine wisdom. This is your season to harvest!

I know that you may be going through some emotional changes that may feel uncomfortable but know that is normal. Your mind is not used to receiving the truth of who you really are and who God is. For a long time, you have been living in a

This is your season to harvest!

cave of lies. Internally your mind, will, and emotions are feeling resistance because it wants to go back to its original fallen nature, but that's not going to happen. Even if externally people and situations are seeking to get you back into that cave that we initially spoke about, that will not be your future. The time that you have invested in doing the work outlined in each chapter before this one is evident. You should be seeing the fruits of the spirit: love, joy, peace, patience, kindness, goodness, faithfulness, gentleness, and self-control manifest. You are looking more and more like Jesus everyday.

At present, individuals around you are noticing the transformations you have undergone. They are looking for the authenticity of your experience. If they determine that it is the real thing, it will either repel them or ignite their curiosity.

As a result, you will add value by showcasing the magnificence of God through your improved and exceptional self. In the end, you become a promotional platform for Christ, which will encourage others to discover the liberation they can experience through Jesus Christ.

What happens next?

While being a living witness for God is a great thing, the most impactful outcome is what happens in private. This is because when your family, close friends, spouse, and children can testify about your journey towards liberation, it becomes very meaningful. It's easy to maintain excellence and integrity in a church, but when you're alone, things can be different. Therefore, what you're doing right now is critical. This is because you're starting from the inside out, not the outside in.

It all starts with loving yourself, dedicating time to yourself, and fighting against the things that try to disqualify you. You are now more familiar with yourself. You're no longer giving up the best outcomes that God has for you, and you're no longer submitting to a poverty mentality. Instead, you now have the mind of Christ, and your achievements reflect the Holy Spirit's powerful work in your life. You have gotten qualitative results that have been signed, sealed and delivered by Him. Here's a strategy to keep the **RESULTS** that you've acquired after reading this book.

The acronym for the word result is the following:

> ➤ Resistance - being able to discipline self to stay focused on a goal.

> ➤ Empowerment - having the stamina and self-determination to maintain a posture of faith.

> ➤ Spirituality - accepting the guidance of the Holy Spirit.

> ➤ Unity - accepting the help of others.

> ➤ Love - making the decision to value yourself and others.

> ➤ Trust - operating in the assured reliance on the character, ability, and strength of God and self.

I believe that the results you obtain with these ingredients lead you to total surrender to God and brings transformation to your life. The Bible says that we are created in his image, He is the Creator of all things, meaning we have the ability to create new things that will attract new results. If you keep getting the same results, that means you are continuously doing something that is producing the same result. Some people are comfortable and have accepted mediocre results because they believe that is all they deserve. But that's not a kingdom principle, Jesus said that He came so that we can live a life of abundance not mediocracy.

What if I tell you that you have a great inheritance through Jesus Christ, one that your mind cannot even imagine? It would be sad to continue living a life getting poor results when you are called to get greater things. God is the only one that makes a way where there is no way. He is the one that enlightens us to be able to make a difference in this world for His glory.

Your progress and achievements are leading you towards a greater understanding of God's nature and character, which is what "glory" means. By allowing the Holy Spirit to guide us, we can continue to transform ourselves to reflect Christ's image. This transformation enables us to seek innovative solutions and ideas for various aspects of life - from businesses to educational systems to communities and beyond. Jesus was a single person who made a significant impact on the world due to the guidance of the Holy Spirit. He influenced 12 people who, in turn, impacted the entire world. Therefore, it's crucial to assess how many people we are reaching and influencing through our accomplishments. In the book "Hello Tomorrow,"[6] Dr. Cindy Trimm speaks about the twelve areas of our lives that we must focus on to have an effective, purposeful life. They are personal identity, companionship, family, personal growth, career, networks, friends and colleagues, recreation and renewal, spiritual growth, financial stability, health and fitness, and personal legacy. I recommend you read it because it lays a firm foundation for the areas you must master to attain your purpose.

To fully embrace your Christian faith, it is crucial to engage in continuous biblical study and read books authored by spiritual leaders. Prioritizing the search for God's truth is imperative for every believer, and learning from these resources can be facilitated by the Holy Spirit. Once you join forces with the Holy Spirit, you will become unstoppable. Reflecting on your journey through previous chapters, you may be amazed at the transformation you have undergone that you never thought possible. With God's power, anything is achievable. The story of Jesus' miraculous healing of a demon-possessed man in Luke 8:26-39 (NIV) highlights the extent of Jesus' power.

---

[6] Trimm, Cindy, *Hello Tomorrow! The Transformational Power of Vision.* Charisma House, 2018.

Let us delve deeper into this passage.

> *They sailed to the region of the Gerasenes,[a] which is across the lake from Galilee. 27 When Jesus stepped ashore, he was met by a demon-possessed man from the town. For a long time this man had not worn clothes or lived in a house, but had lived in the tombs. 28 When he saw Jesus, he cried out and fell at his feet, shouting at the top of his voice, "What do you want with me, Jesus, Son of the Most High God? I beg you, don't torture me!" 29 For Jesus had commanded the impure spirit to come out of the man. Many times it had seized him, and though he was chained hand and foot and kept under guard, he had broken his chains and had been driven by the demon into solitary places. 30 Jesus asked him, "What is your name?"*
>
> *"Legion," he replied, because many demons had gone into him. 31 And they begged Jesus repeatedly not to order them to go into the Abyss.*
>
> *32 A large herd of pigs was feeding there on the hillside. The demons begged Jesus to let them go into the pigs, and he gave them permission. 33 When the demons came out of the man, they went into the pigs, and the herd rushed down the steep bank into the lake and was drowned.*
>
> *34 When those tending the pigs saw what had happened, they ran off and reported this in the town and countryside, 35 and the people went out to see what had happened. When they came to Jesus, they found the man from whom the demons had gone out, sitting at Jesus' feet, dressed and in his right mind; and they were afraid.*

In this passage, the demoniac got instantaneous relief and results from our merciful Savior. I shared this because I wanted you to get an understanding of the length Jesus will go to bring healing, redemption, and restoration in your life.

Don't let fear stop you from getting your blessing!

Notice in the last part of the previous passage it says, …and they were afraid. The miracle Jesus performed was mind blowing. Sometimes when we face the impossible becoming the possible, fear will try to steal it away from us.

> *⁴ Even though I walk through the darkest valley,[a] I will fear no evil, for you are with me; your rod and your staff, they comfort me.*

PSALM 23:4 (NIV)

It is common to feel scared about the outcomes we achieve as they could result in rejection from our loved ones. Some individuals may not comprehend their purpose and may attempt to downplay their abilities and the resources given to them by God. It is essential to acknowledge that not everyone will attain the same results as you if you remain obedient. Some people may continue to experience failure because they keep repeating the same actions, expecting different outcomes – as famously noted by Albert Einstein: "Insanity is doing the same thing over and over again, expecting different results." Attempting to achieve different results through repetitive practices is not feasible. Changing your habits may lead to positive changes in your life, but it requires patience. Remember you have lived with these habits for a long time, and when you start changing these habits one step at a time, you will experience resistance. But, when self-determination and discipline kicks in, you are well on your way to getting a better result.

Do the work necessary for the best version of you to be available to God to fulfill your purpose.

God's purpose is waiting for you to be ready, internally and externally. Purpose has a partnership with the Holy Spirit, and if you fulfill the prerequisites by doing the internal cleansing and building a strong biblical foundation necessary in preparation for the next level, you will be well on your way to fulfilling your call from God.

Remember, you and the Holy Spirit are a team.

When you grow through your relationship and partnership with the Holy Spirit, you will start attracting the things you need to realize your purpose. When I started this journey, I started attracting certain kinds of people, and my circle was changing. I was initially surrounded by people that seemed to have no identity; they did not know where they were headed. They were people pleasers and did not have any hope or desire to become leaders. I would notice their lukewarm demeanor and they had no plans for future success or promotion.

When the Lord continued to work in me, I realized that I had to change the circle. Some of the individuals were comfortable with their status, but I felt that was not what my future looked like. One day, the Holy Spirit was speaking to me and making me uncomfortable with the circle I was in. I ignored His prompting until something bad happened. God has a way of doing things when He sees that you are not where you are supposed to be. He sees the intention of your heart and what you are doing, but something is blocking the way, and He can remove things in our lives that no longer serve His purpose. I decided to change my circle and, in the process, received a lot of rejection and criticism. When all else does not make sense, you have to trust God's process.

Sometimes progress is preceded by persecution.

For our struggle is not against flesh and blood, but against the rulers, against the authorities, against the powers of this dark world and against the spiritual forces of evil in the heavenly realms.

EPHESIANS 6:12 (NIV)

Often persecution is a sign that the pursuit of your purpose is bringing a change to the atmosphere around you. Sometimes when that happens, it attracts oppression. That is why when you are making decisions along the way, trust where God is taking you. The beauty of allowing the Holy Spirit to guide you is that He knows what areas you should be working on because He has the spiritual blueprint for your life. One day, when I was in my office studying my bible, I remember hearing the subtle voice of the Holy Spirit. He said, "This is the year that I take you out of the anonymous." Wow! Soon after I started to receive invitations to bless other ministries. I just could not believe it! I just wanted people to see God through me. I wanted them to know him more and the truth about the Gospel.

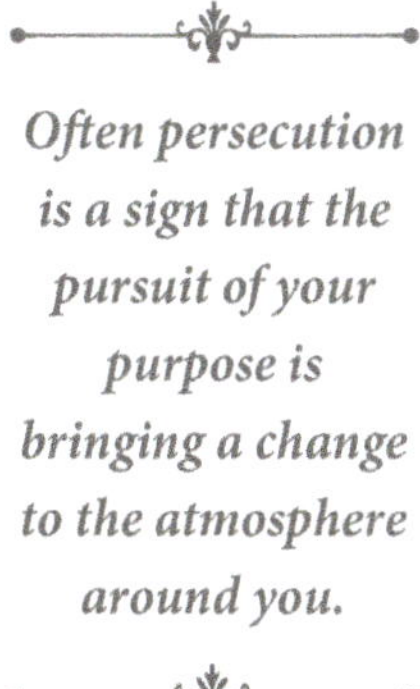

Often persecution is a sign that the pursuit of your purpose is bringing a change to the atmosphere around you.

The message of the Gospel breathes true life into you. When you truly believe and begin a personal relationship with the heavenly Father through repentance and faith in Christ, the Holy Spirit takes up residence inside of you. Salvation is granted; sin is forgiven. Your new life has begun. Having a personal relationship with God through Jesus Christ is life changing.

When God is responsible for the results you have birthed, he will equip you to protect it from the destiny assassins. A destiny assassin is a spirit that is assigned to come against your purpose. Its objective is to paralyze you through fear, doubt, deception, and many other strategies that it believes will work based on your areas of vulnerability.

You must stay connected God to protect the results you have obtained. As you continue getting results, you will need to continue praying and seeking Him to preserve the results you have obtained. Prayer is the survival skill you will need to utilize in order to survive.

In a confused world, you are constantly in a battle to maintain the ground you won during your spiritual transformation. You may believe that you can protect it with your own strength, but something so powerful as the results you are obtaining needs a supernatural force to keep it intact. The Bible says:

> [19] *They will fight against you but will not overcome you, for I am with you and will rescue you," declares the* LORD.
>
> **JEREMIAH 1:19 (NIV)**

Jesus Christ has enabled me to be victorious in fighting my persona battles. This is the blessing benefit of placing your trust in Him in everything you do. Why? Because if He is the Alpha and Omega, beginning and end, that means whatever he starts, he will finish. When you feel the attack, resist and trust God. You must trust that he is with you along the way, even if it feels like you are alone. You are not alone if you have placed him first.

You will be tested!

In order to ensure its legitimacy, the outcome that you achieve will undergo testing. It is important to recognize that anything entrusted to God will be evaluated for its quality. As the creator, God always ensures the goodness of his creations. This is evident in Genesis 1 where he took a break to appreciate the goodness of his work. Despite this, what may appear good to God may not necessarily be seen as such by humans. The world we live in often perceives what is good as bad and vice versa. Therefore, when positive outcomes manifest, people may question its validity and inquire if the process was followed diligently or if shortcuts were taken. Opting for shortcuts may impede long-term and permanent results. To receive the manifestation of the Holy Spirit in your life, it is imperative to yield completely to God's will. Merely doing something halfway may give you temporary outcomes, but God intends to bring about a complete transformation within you so that you can fulfill your purpose. His desire is for you to achieve lasting results that will contribute to the advancement of His kingdom. By prioritizing your personal growth, you will experience an overflow of blessings that others won't be able to disregard. The Holy Spirit is our greatest ally in this journey. Avoid relying solely on your own comprehension, as it won't lead you to the eternal outcomes you aspire for.

These results not only have the ability to help others but also to leave a legacy for the next generation. When God creates something from scratch it is eternal. He not only wants to bless the now, but He also wants to bless your tomorrow, and the future. He wants you to stay focused on continuously working on yourself and growing through his word and yield continuously to the Holy Spirit. Sometimes, people are inspired by your results, and they attempt to follow your method and they obtain the same results which is an extension of your purpose. For example, the prophet Elijah was the mentor for Elisha, and he ended up with a double portion of the anointing of his mentor. God's purpose for our lives is often multiplied through others with a similar anointing. The more God's children get results, the more the Kingdom of God expands.

See, it's not about us; it is about Him in us. Once we have Him, we have it all.

Your result is not for selfish hearts; it is for hearts that love God above all things and love people.

CHAPTER 7

METAMORPHOSIS

Well done, you have gained an understanding of the significance of discovering your purpose and following it. Purpose can be defined as a goal or objective to be achieved, as per Merriam Webster Dictionary. Although our literary journey has come to an end, your pursuit of fulfilling your purpose will continue until you reach Heaven or the return of Jesus. It is a privilege to serve God wholeheartedly, with a renewed mind and soul.

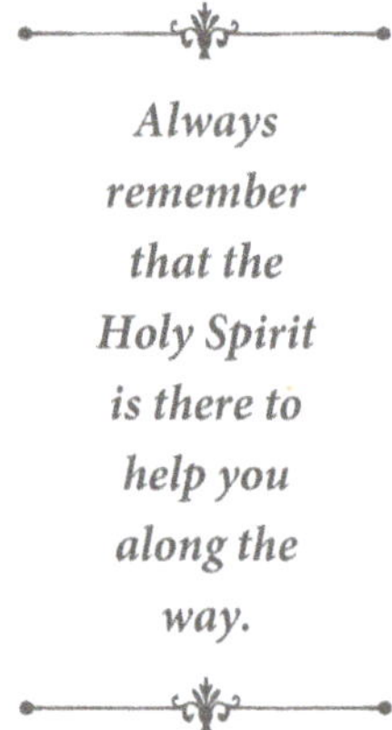

Always remember that the Holy Spirit is there to help you along the way.

At this point, you should have a good understanding of your purpose and the plans that God has for you. It's important to remember that knowing your purpose is only half the battle - understanding how to fulfill that purpose is just as crucial. While many people prioritize starting an assignment, it's completing it that truly matters. Don't let regret consume you later in life by failing to act on your purpose.

Remember, faith without action is meaningless. So get to work and fulfill your purpose! Someone out there is counting on you to take action, so allow the Spirit of God to move you. If you find yourself stuck, turn to our Heavenly Father for guidance and revelation.

Even Jesus himself sought the full revelation of his assignment by fasting and spending time in the desert. This allowed him to receive the necessary instructions for a successful ministry. Always remember that the Holy Spirit is there to help you along the way.

Let's do a quick review of what we covered in the previous chapters.

Chapter 1- Cave of the Mind

> ➢ Identified some of the good and bad things that happened in your life.
>
> ➢ Examined how these things shaped who you are.
>
> ➢ Examined the truth for God's abundant provision for hope, faith and love in your life.

Chapter 2- The Why

> ➢ You came to the understanding that you will need the help of the Holy Spirit.
>
> ➢ You came to the understanding that you will need to be refocused in some areas of your life.

Chapter 3- A Plan of Breakthrough

> ➢ You must choose a place of refuge/secret place.
>
> ➢ You must position yourself to be empowered.
>
> ➢ You must see life as a temporary time to leave permanent footprints for others.

Chapter 4-Detoxification

> ➢ You need to feel safe and at peace letting go of the unnecessary to receive the necessary things.
>
> ➢ Acknowledge that detoxification is worth the process.
>
> ➢ Through the journey, envision your future and use it as a motivator during the difficult times.

Chapter 5- Application

> ➤ When we ask for the help of the Holy Spirit, the impossible becomes possible.

> ➤ Emotional resistance is overcome through faith in God.

> ➤ Seek to become spiritually, emotionally, mentally, physically, and socially healthy.

Chapter 6-Results

> ➤ You are in control of your results, if you do so with a healthy mindset, you will get good results.

> ➤ Work on stability, consistency, perseverance, and believe in the transformation.

> ➤ Freely give back to others what you have been given.

Chapter 7- Metamorphosis

> ➤ You can transform others through the transformational power that is within you.

> ➤ You are the light that can shine to bring others to the truth of who they really are.

> ➤ You become a vessel of God to transfer people from death to life.

Once you grasp the significance of your path, you develop a resolute determination to strive towards satisfaction, which in turn will assist others on their pilgrimage in discovering the Kingdom of God. Your compliance will always have a far-reaching impact in the realm of the divine. When you are abundantly blessed, you have the ability to bestow blessings upon others. You become the driving force for a transformation in the kingdom.

What does metamorphosis mean?

Let's take a look at Merriam Webster Dictionary's definition of metamorphosis: a change of physical form, structure, or substance especially by supernatural means or: a striking alteration in appearance, character, or circumstances.[7] Your personal metamorphosis starts when you connect to the power invested in you by God. You are God's masterpiece. When you start on your journey to purpose, that gets God's attention! God is the ultimate creator and knows what to change in you and what He has created you to change. The Holy Spirit directs you to where you should invest your time. God is a perfect God. He knows exactly what tools you will need for your specific assignment. Keep in mind that you are not called to help everyone in this world, and that's okay. The more you rely on the wise counsel of the Holy Spirit and place your faith, obedience, and trust in Him, the more clarity you will get.

Now you know that to go through this powerful metamorphosis, you must operate under a supernatural power that gives you the ability to overcome cultural strongholds, erroneous beliefs, alienating opinions, etc. What does supernatural power actually mean? Supernatural power is the power of God that makes impossible things possible. When this takes place in an individual, it creates a divine power source that is activated by the Holy Spirit, with the intent to bring a spiritual transformation. As you continue this amazing journey that does not end when this book ends, you will be part of the miracles that God uses to transform the lives of others because you are impregnated with the solution.

---

[7]https://www.merriam-webster.com/dictionary/metamorphosis (https://www.merriam-webster.com/dictionary/metamorphosis

People that carry solutions gain value, and that value has a source. The source of everything good is God and He sent the Holy Spirit to help us do good in the Earth. We just need to say *yes* to God.

> *Teach me to do Your will, For You are my God; Your Spirit is good.*
> *Lead me in the land of uprightness.*
>
> **PSALM 143:10 (NKJV)**

Here, we can see the willingness of the Holy Spirit to teach us the will of God for our lives. First, we recognize that His will is better than our own will. We have seen this through our past experiences. How long have we tried to live life on our own and have been unsuccessful?

We have made impulsive decisions that have affected our personal life and those that we love. We have done our own will for too long, and our own will has brought undesired consequences that have pressured us to enter a dark cave.

You must acknowledge God's prominence and place Him on the throne of your heart. Believe that the spirit of God knows what is good for you. He knows the power of walking in God's will. Walking in the will of God brings peace that surpasses all understanding because you know you are walking on purpose.

Don't be afraid of the changes taking place in your life, be afraid of not changing. Don't be afraid of encountering the real you; be afraid of not living in the abundant will of God.

You have been transformed!

To clarify who you are, let's take a look at *Ephesians 1*:

Ephesians 1:1
I am a saint.

Ephesians 1:3
I am blessed with every spiritual blessing in Christ.

Ephesians 1:4-5
I am chosen and predestined for the adoption of sonship by the Heavenly Father.

Ephesians 1:6
I am accepted by God and a recipient of his grace.

Ephesians 1:7
I am redeemed and forgiven in Christ.

Ephesians 1:11
I have a wonderful inheritance of spiritual riches in Christ.

Ephesians 1:13-14
I am indwelled and sealed by the Holy Spirit, who guarantees my inclusion into the family of God.

Ephesians 1:15-18
I have access to spiritual wisdom and insight in Christ by the Holy Spirit.

Ephesians 1:19-21
I participate in the resurrection and ascension of Christ because of the power of the indwelling Holy Spirit.

Ephesians 1:22-23
As a member of the Body of Christ, I am united to the Lord and represent him on earth.

The bible conveys the message of how we are made wonderfully by God and have great worth as His creation. It also highlights the fact that God's love for us is shown through the sacrifice of His only son, Jesus, who silently endured the journey to the cross to fulfill His purpose. God's word emphasizes that a true sign of fulfilling one's purpose is the increasing pressure felt and the supernatural ability to endure persecution without complaint.

In summary, the bible celebrates the beauty of God's creation and the sacrificial love shown through Jesus' journey to fulfill His purpose. It also acknowledges the supernatural strength required to withstand persecution without complaint as a sign of purposeful living. The bible says this is accomplished,

Not by might, nor by power, but by my spirit, saith the LORD of hosts.

ZECHARIAH 4:6B (KJV)

This scripture highlights the significance of the Holy Spirit in the metamorphic process. The story of Jesus demonstrates his extraordinary resilience and conviction in his mission, which he knew would ultimately benefit others. The process of personal growth and development not only equips us with new knowledge and tools but also enables us to help others who are going through similar experiences. Our struggles and tears are not in vain but rather serve as an investment towards someone else's recovery. When we witness others overcoming their challenges, it brings us joy and helps us appreciate how Jesus' suffering and death led to the salvation of billions of people.

Jesus had a cave experience!

After the Sabbath, at dawn on the first day of the week, Mary Magdalene and the other Mary went to look at the tomb. 2 There was a violent earthquake, for an angel of the Lord came down from heaven and, going to the tomb, rolled back the stone and sat on it. 3 His appearance was like lightning, and his clothes were white as snow. 4 The guards were so afraid of him that they shook and became like dead men.5 The angel said to the women, "Do not be afraid, for I know that you are looking for Jesus, who was crucified. 6 He is not here; he has risen, just as he said. Come and see the place where he lay.

MATTHEW 28:1 - 6 (NIV)

"He is not here; he has risen," were the words that the angel said to the women that were looking for Jesus Christ in the tomb after the three days following his death. The story of Jesus Christ's resurrection from the tomb is truly amazing, and it also applies to your life. It's inspiring to see how the women returned to the tomb to find that Jesus was no longer there. This story represents the fact that people may check back on you to see if you're still stuck in the same place, but they'll be surprised to find that you've moved on.

You can now enjoy the freedom that comes with being released from the cave that held you back from pursuing your goals. You can use your transformation to help others and show them the power of Jesus Christ's resurrection. With a clear sense of purpose, you can navigate this confusing world and make a positive impact. Through the Holy Spirit, you can help others experience the same transformation that you've gone through. The tomb is now empty! Who is NEXT!

Things got tough for Jesus before He had His cave experience.

During a moment of inner turmoil, I struggled with the unfair accusations against my character and reputation. Despite my pure intentions, I felt misunderstood and hurt. In an effort to find solace, I turned to meditation and was led by the Holy Spirit to watch a scene from the movie, The Passion of Christ, depicting Jesus' persecution and eventual crucifixion. As I watched, I was moved to tears by the realization that those whom Jesus loved and came to help were the same ones who rejected Him, yet He remained silent throughout His suffering. Witnessing His pain and torture affected me deeply, and I felt a heavy weight on my heart. Despite the agony, Jesus never complained because He knew it was His calling. Although some may be deterred by the notion that following in His footsteps may lead to persecution and rejection, I found comfort in His unwavering commitment to His purpose.

Imagine that you are viewing the movie. As Jesus is going through all this, we can see ourselves in this movie clip. How many times have you felt rejected by the people you truly love and helped? How many times have you been misinterpreted or misunderstood? How many times have you been judged? How many times have you not been accepted for who you are? Jesus was not accepted nor received from those he was called to save, meaning that we will also go through some of the same things that He did to walk in our purpose. No one said purpose is easy to walk in, but through Christ, it is possible to embrace. We see numerous examples of the people of God in the Bible maturing spiritually in order to walk in their divine purpose, and you can too!

Remember to always trust in God and keep your mind stayed on Him!

It is crucial to have faith and trust in God, especially in the process of discovering your purpose, as you will encounter Him in a unique way.

You may face challenges and opposition during this journey, but it will all be worth it in the end. These obstacles are a battle of the mind, which means that you are making progress. Just like an athlete who faces resistance from their opponents during a soccer game, you will also face resistance from your enemy as you step out of the darkness and walk with a renewed mind and Christ-like authority. Setting your mind on the things of the flesh is death, but to set your mind on the things of the Spirit is life and peace.

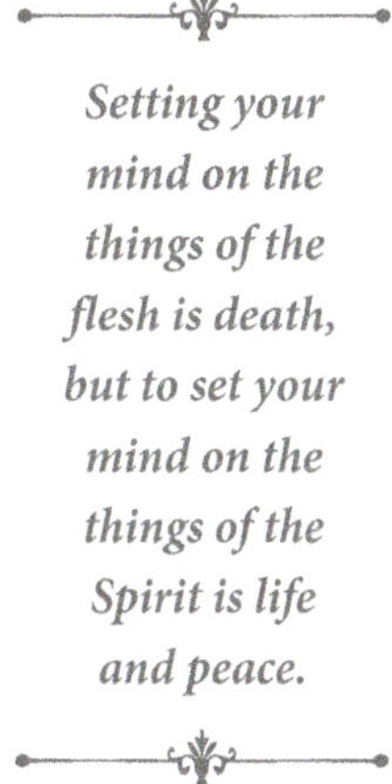

By focusing on things that are true, reputable, authentic, beautiful, and praiseworthy, you are taking control of your identity and defeating your opponent.

The mind governed by the flesh is death, but the mind governed by the Spirit is life and peace.

ROMANS 8:6 (NIV)

This isn't the end of my story and it's not the end of yours.

I emerged from a period of darkness with the help of the Lord, whom I trusted to guide my life. My experience of being in a difficult situation improved when I sought His help. I had faith in Him and His plans for me and my loved ones. I overcame my struggles and now encourage others to do the same. I have gained a new perspective and am now able to positively impact the world. It's important to stay focused on your purpose and not get lost in the confusion of the world. Remember that this is just the beginning of your journey and it's important to stay connected with supportive people and continue to have faith in God. He can bring unexpected surprises just like He did for me. Embrace the new version of yourself and inspire others to do the same, so that you can say like the Apostle Paul, *I have fought the good fight, I have finished the race, I have kept the faith.* (2 Timothy 4:7 NIV) You are a winner!

THE SALVATION PRAYER

Lord Jesus, I know that I am a sinner, and I ask you for Your forgiveness. I believe You died for my sins and was resurrected from the dead. I voluntarily turn from my sins and invite You to come into my heart. I want to trust You as my Lord and Savior and commit to follow You all the days of my life from now and forever more. Amen.

ABOUT THE AUTHOR

Zuleyka Salazar is a woman chosen by God who has a strong desire to help those who are suffering and in need of healing. She spreads positivity and joy to the world through the various ministries, organizations, and businesses that have been bestowed upon her through God's grace. Along with being a co-founder of the Eternal Life Embassy in Lorton, VA, she is also a highly sought-after speaker at conferences, a specialist in empowerment, and a transformational leader who has a unique ability to guide people towards their purpose. She has been called by God to bring salvation, restoration, and the message of God's love to people all over the world.

www.ingramcontent.com/pod-product-compliance
Lightning Source LLC
Chambersburg PA
CBHW050008040726
47599CB00014B/1267